RHYTHMICAL IMPROVISATION AND THE BLUES

for Piano and keyboards

Daniel Spiegelberg

Contact the author: spiegeldan76@gmail.com

Copyright © 2017

All rights reserved. No part of this publication may be reproduced, stored in a retrieval system, or transmitted, in any form or by any means, electronic, mechanical, photocopying, recording, or otherwise, without the prior written permission of the author.

ISBN 978-0-692-83296-7

Book overview -

The example songs in this book utilize the major and minor blues scales to create the right hand melody and solo lines. Other non-scale tones are then periodically introduced to add variety and interest. The example songs come in two different stylistic sounds – some blues and others – a sound that leans towards pop/jazz. All of the tunes are in the twelve bar blues format. The left hand accompaniment chords used in the example songs are kept rhythmically simple in the beginning but then slowly increase in rhythmical difficulty as the book progresses. Developing independence and syncopation between the right and left hands are a main goal in this book. Other focal points are -

- Left hand chord shells and rootless comping chords
- Creating riffs and melodies from rhythms
- Creating a blues song from scratch
- Over 50 twelve bar blues song examples
- Suggested fingerings are provided

Harmonizing the melodic line, double-stops, grace notes, trills, approach tones, passing tones, and enclosures are also covered.

How to use this book –

I highly recommend using a metronome while playing through the tunes in this book. A metronome will help you keep a steady tempo. If at any time you have difficulty playing one of the examples in this book try not to get discouraged. I have tried to make the exercises as palatable as possible but depending upon your current playing ability you may find some tunes harder to play than others. Follow this formula anytime you struggle with an exercise or tune:

1. Slow the tune down – way down if necessary. If that doesn't work go to step two.

2. Learn each hand separately – practice the right hand melody all by itself until you have mastered it. Then learn the left hand accompaniment all by itself. Then slowly play hands together. One measure at a time if necessary.

3. And finally, bring the song up to a reasonable tempo (tempo markings are provided on each tune).

Occasionally, you may find that the above formula isn't helping either. In that case, **skip the tune or exercise for now and come back to it at a later time.**

This book should be considered an intermediate level. Some level of reading is necessary most of which is in the right hand melodies. No prior knowledge of playing the blues is necessary as the book starts from the ground up. Some knowledge of music theory is always helpful but the book will give you most of what you need. I have provided fingerings for the entire book however, not all hands are the same (or the same size). Those new to the blues probably stand to get the most out of the fingerings. That being said, if they help use them (at least some of them). Once you have chosen the fingering you are going to use for a particular passage I suggest penciling in those fingerings.

I got a lot of enjoyment (not to mention challenge) in writing this book. I hope this book will help you in pursuit of your musical goals.

TABLE OF CONTENTS

                          page

1. The basics ………………………………………………………………….4

2. Left hand accompaniment ……………………………………………...9

3. The major blues scale ……………………………………………………14

4. Combining scales and comp chords…………………………………16

5. Improvising basics………………………………………………………...20

6. Riff placement …………………………………………………………....26

7. Creating a blues…………………………………………………………...31

8. More twelve bar examples……………………………………………..32

9. Playing with backing tracks……………………………………………52

10. Other notes to use with the major blues scale…………………………..53

11. The minor blues scale……………………………………………………61

12. Other notes to use with the minor blues scale…………………………..72

13. Adding harmony to the melodic line…………………………………82

14. Putting it all together……………………………………………………...92

15. Scale warm-up ideas……………………………………………………101

16. Playing in other keys……………………………………………………104

17. Appendix…………………………………………………………………..124

CHAPTER 1 - THE BASICS

INTERVALS

An interval is the vertical distance between two notes. A half step interval is the smallest of intervals. On a piano it is two keys that are next to each other i.e. there are no other keys between them. A whole step interval is equal to a distance of two half steps (1/2 step + 1/2 step = 1 whole step). One way to describe an interval is by the number of half steps and whole steps that separate two notes:

Example intervals

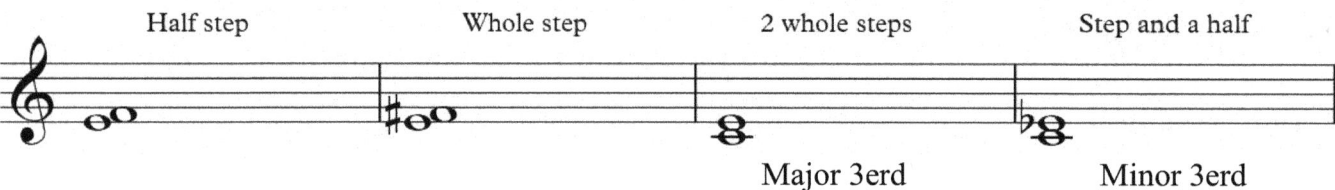

The intervals in the last two measures are also known as a major and minor third respectively (as indicated below the staff).

THE MAJOR SCALE

The major scale consists of seven notes that have an interval code of - whole step, whole step, half step, whole step, whole step, whole step, half step. The first note of a scale is referred to as the tonic and is the same note in which the scale is named after. The numbers below the staff indicate scale degrees:

C major scale

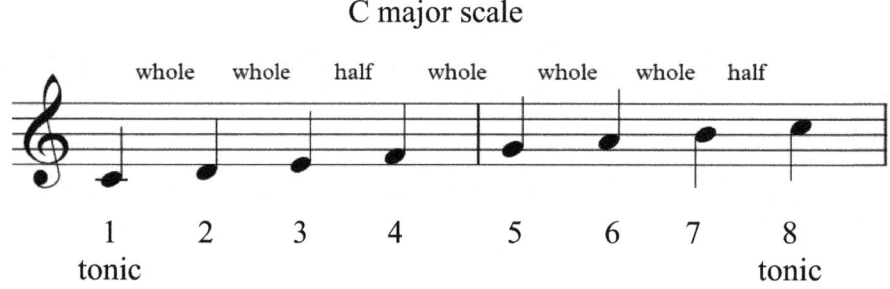

THE MINOR SCALE

Every major scale has a relative minor scale associated with it. To find the relative minor scale of any major scale simply go down one-and-a-half steps from the tonic. That note is the new tonic of the relative minor scale. As an example - to find the relative minor scale of C major simply go down one and a half steps from the tonic (C). This note is A. Therefore, the A minor scale is the relative minor of the C major scale. Notice that the notes of the C major and A minor scales are the same. Only the starting note (tonic) is different. This creates a new interval code, as well (as it relates to the new tonic):

A minor scale

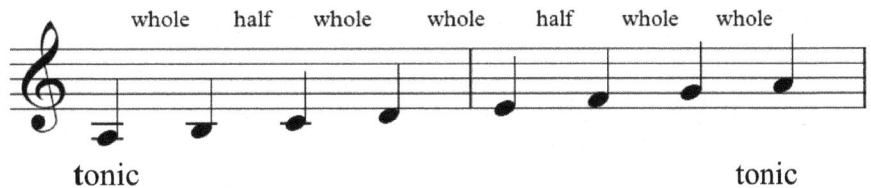

tonic   tonic

HARMONY - THE 4 MAIN CHORD TYPES

Major triad – consists of a root, major third, and a fifth:

C major triad

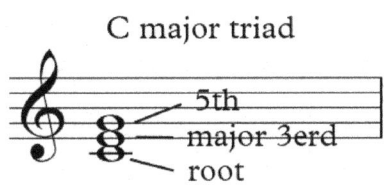

Minor triad – consists of a root, minor third, and a fifth:

C minor triad

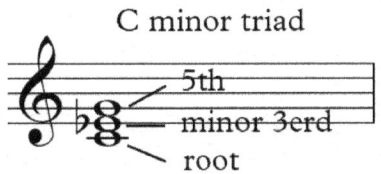

Diminished triad – consists of a root, minor third, and a flatted (diminished) fifth:

C diminished

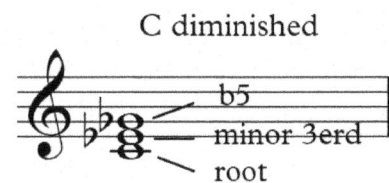

Dominant seven chord – is a four note chord that consists of a root, major third, fifth, and flat seven:

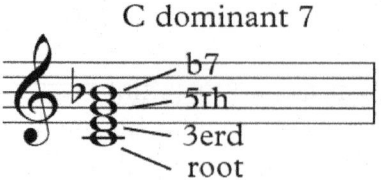

TRIADS ASSOCIATED WITH THE MAJOR SCALE

A major scale has seven diatonic triads associated with it. Referred to as - diatonic - because the triads only use notes that are part of the scale. Chords are often shown using roman numerals indicating which degree of the scale the chord is on and what type of chord it is (major, minor, etc.). A lower case roman numeral indicating minor and upper case major:

Diatonic triads associated with the C major scale

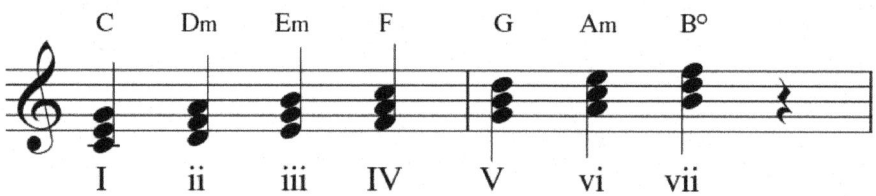

CHORD EXTENSIONS

Any triad can have more notes added to it. These are called chord extensions and can include the 7th, 9th, 11th, and 13th:

Added extensions starting with a C major triad

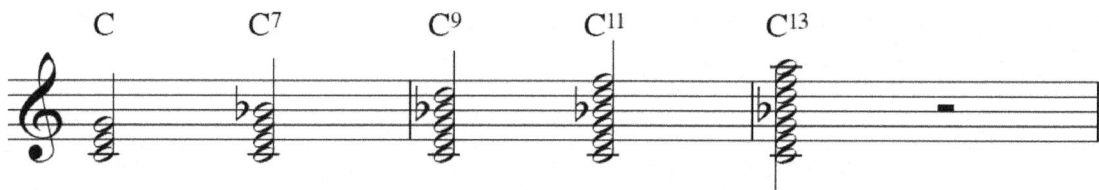

Added extensions starting with a C minor triad

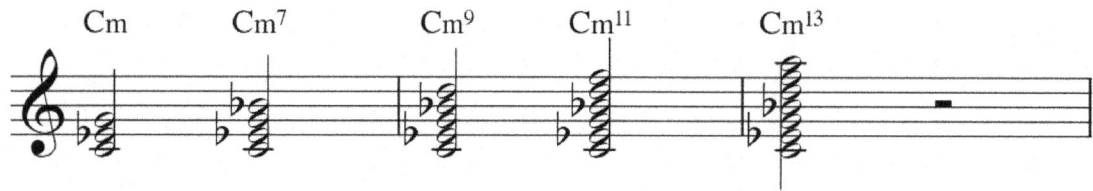

RHYTHM - THE BLUES FEEL

Most pop and rock music are based on an eighth note rhythmical feel. It is played as written:

Blues and jazz, on the other hand, are based on a triplet swing feel. This swing feel can be notated in the music literally or with straight eighth notes that are played (interpreted) with a triplet feel:

Often written like this…   but played like this.

THE TWELVE BAR BLUES FORM

The twelve bar blues is a twelve bar song that is repeated. Below is a common twelve bar blues in the key of C showing the chords and associated roman numerals. Notice that only three chords are used for the entire progression. Each chord being a <u>dominant 7 chord</u> type:

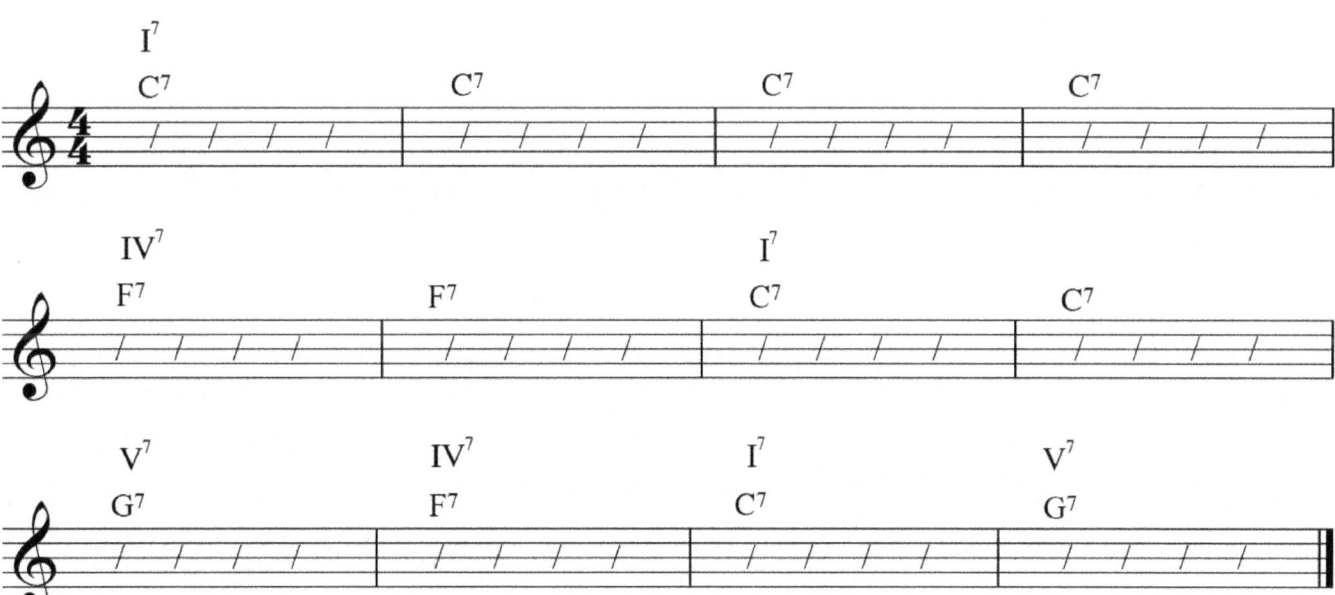

Here is another example in the key of F. Notice in the second measure that the chord changes to the IV⁷ chord. It is a common practice in the blues to go to the IV⁷ chord in the second measure. This is referred to as a quick four:

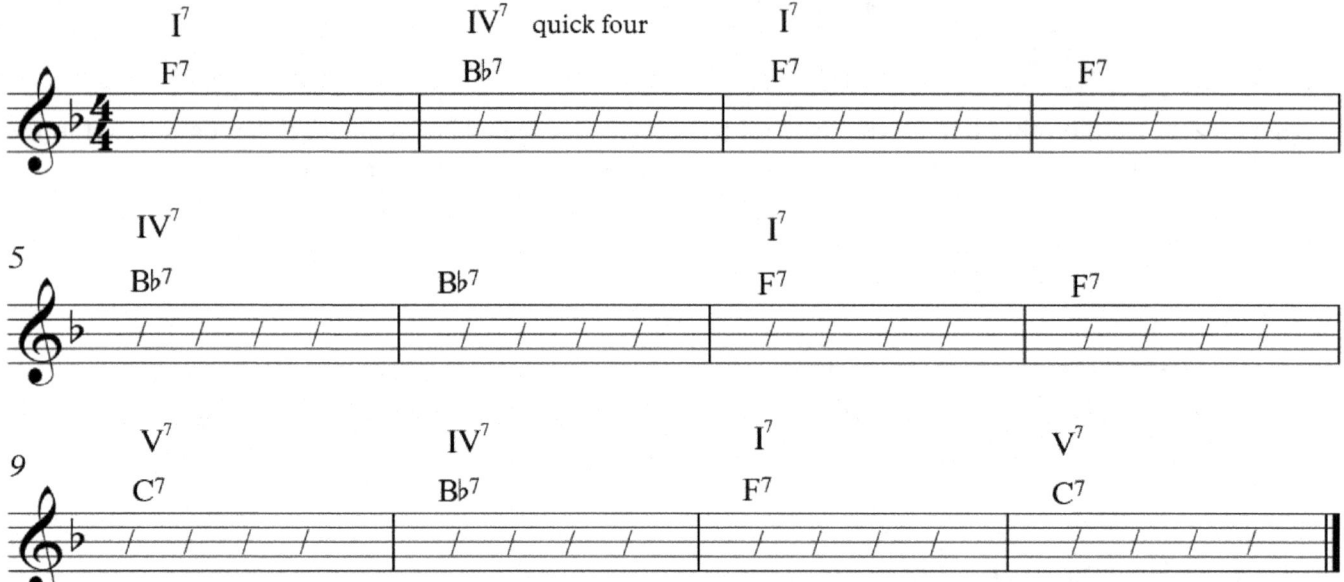

CHAPTER 2 - LEFT HAND ACCOMPANIMENT

A word that is often used to describe a piano accompaniment is <u>comping</u>. For all practical purposes, the word comping simply means to <u>accompany</u>. This could mean playing chords along-side of a vocalist or soloing instrumentalist but it can also mean adding left hand chords for your right hand solo's (or melodies). You are, in the latter case, accompanying yourself.

Left hand comp chords are derived from these basic <u>block chords</u> –

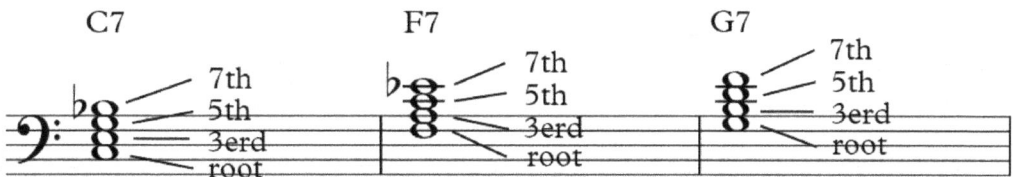

This is the same as above except F7 and G7 are lowered one octave –

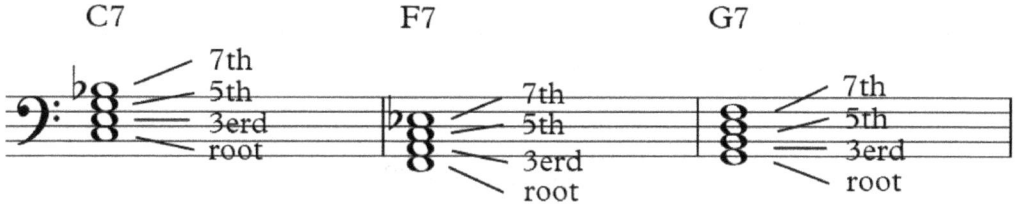

3 WAYS TO FORM COMP CHORDS IN THE LEFT HAND

1. Rooted shells – A rooted chord shell is a two note chord that has the root as its lowest note and one other note from the basic block chord. The most common way to do this is to play the root and the 7th –

Play only the root and 7th

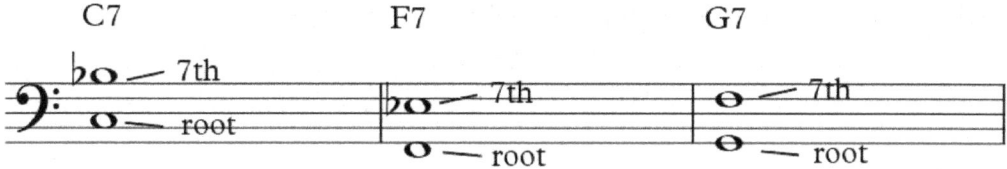

2. Guide tones – playing guide tones means that you are only playing the third and seventh of the chord. The root and 5th have been removed. Guide tones can be played in either <u>form A</u> or <u>form B</u>. In <u>form A</u> the 3erd is the lower of the two notes. In <u>form B</u> the interval is inverted and the 7th is the lower note –

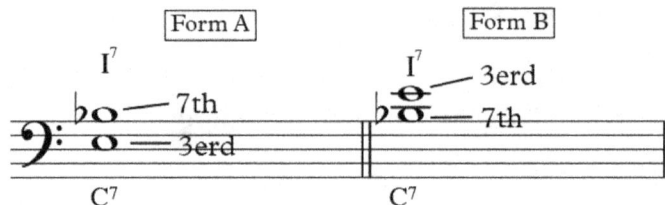

When using guide tones in the left hand to play through a twelve bar blues the IV^7 and V^7 chords will always be the <u>opposite form</u> than what the I^7 chord is. If the I^7 chord is in <u>form A</u> than both the IV^7 and V^7 chords will be in <u>form B</u>. The inverse of this is also true. **Also** – a blues chord progression that starts in <u>form A</u> is called <u>chord sequence A</u>. A chord progression that starts in <u>form B</u> is called <u>chord sequence B</u>. Play through each sequence and notice how little your left hand needs to move when changing chords –

<u>Guide tones used in sequence A</u>

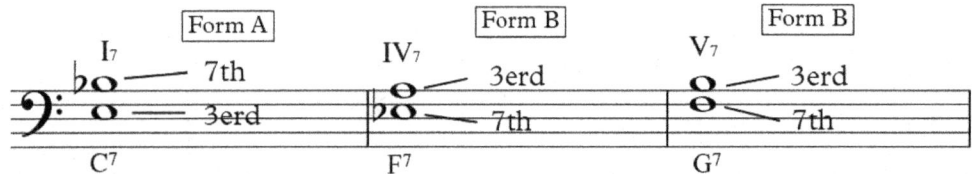

<u>Guide tones used in sequence B</u>

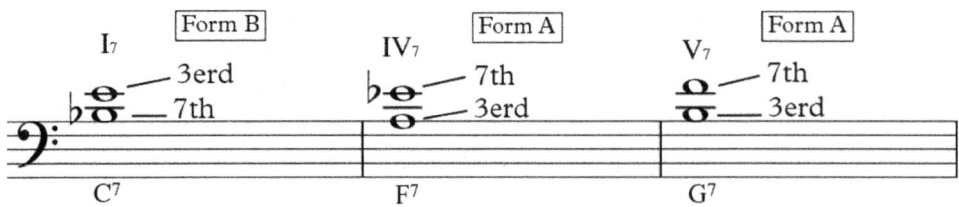

3. Rootless comping chords – if we take the guide tones (3rd and 7th) and add one <u>extended note</u>, we end up with a rootless comping chord. Called rootless because they have no root. **It is very common to play these kinds of chords in blues and jazz while the bass player plays the roots for you.** Bear in mind, that by themselves, these chords may sound somewhat empty. In upcoming chapters, however, we will begin to add-in the right hand and that familiar jazz/blues sound will become very apparent. Play the following chords (one at a time) with your right hand while adding the root bass note with the left. This will allow you to hear what these chords sound like with the root added. **<u>Chord sequence A should be memorized as it will be the main sequence used in this book</u>** –

Rootless comping chords used in sequence A

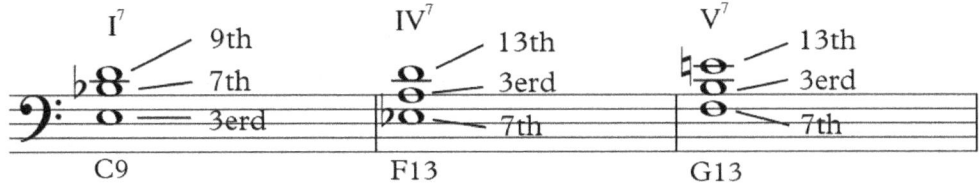

Rootless comping chords used in sequence B
(3/7 guide tones are inverted)

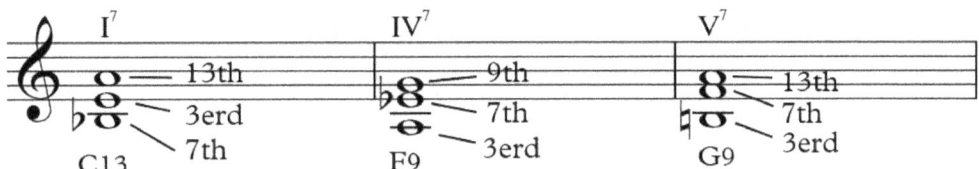

LEFT HAND COMPING CHORD EXERCISE

Play through the following 12 bar blues with the left hand. Rootless comping chord sequence 'A' is utilized –

Track 1

COMPING RHYTHMS

In the last twelve bar example the comping rhythms were kept simple by playing half notes on beats one and three. Here we will explore some more interesting rhythms that would typically be used in jazz and blues. Here are three typical left hand comping rhythms:

TWO HAND COMPING CHORD EXERCISE

In the following exercise, the dot (.) over the chord is a staccato marking which means to play the chord for a very short duration (no sustain). The right hand plays the chord and the left hand plays the bass note. I highly suggest using a metronome or rhythm machine (set to swing beat) when playing the exercises in this book. It will teach you to keep a steady tempo. A tempo setting of between 110 and 120 bpm should be adequate for this exercise. Remember to swing the beat –

Track 2

> **Don't skip this step** – now go back through the exercise again using the left hand to play the chord. Omit the bottom bass note. This is important because you will be using the left hand to play these chords through most of the rest of this book!

CHAPTER THREE - THE MAJOR BLUES SCALE

Now that we have some basic left hand accompaniment chords worked out, it's time to focus on the right hand. The major blues scale is derived from the major pentatonic scale. The major pentatonic scale is derived from the major scale. The numbers below the staff refer to the scale degree –

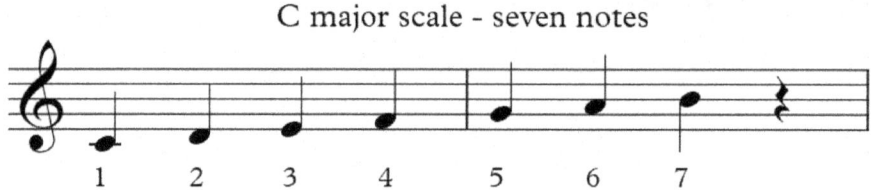

Omit the 4th and 7th degree of the major scale to get the pentatonic scale –

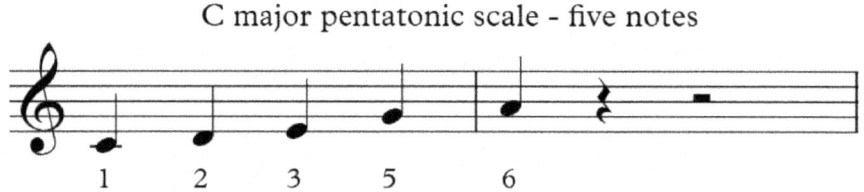

And finally, add the ♭3 to obtain the major blues scale:

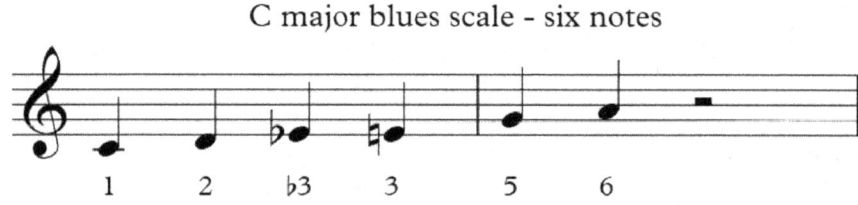

Practice the major blues scale with the right hand as shown in the exercise below. The numbers below the staff give the right hand fingering. Begin playing the scale slowly. As you feel more comfortable with the scale, turn on the metronome. Play the tempo indicated:

♩ = 75-85

Major blues scale – one octave

Track 3

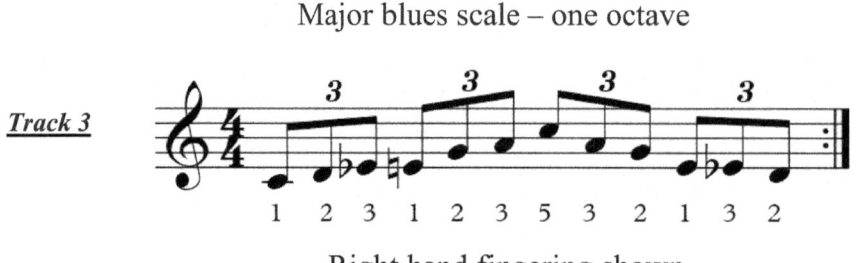

Right hand fingering shown

Now practice the two octave version of the same scale (keep the tempo the same):

Major blues scale – two octaves

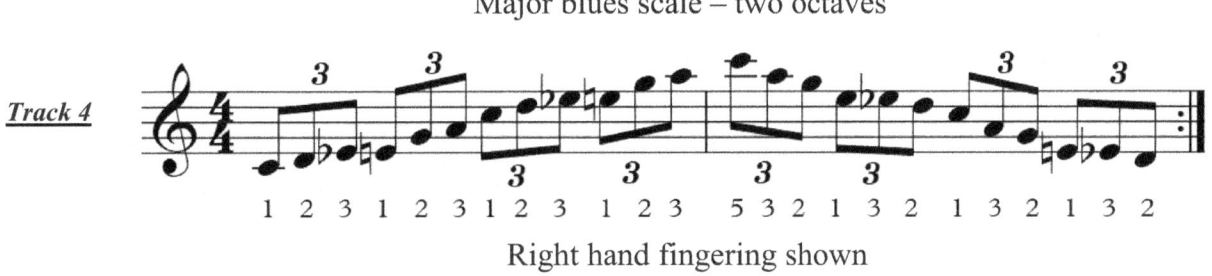

Track 4

Right hand fingering shown

EIGHTH NOTES THAT SWING

Here is another way to practice the C major blues scale using eighth notes. Because you are playing eighth notes you can increase the tempo to that indicated. <u>Remember to swing the eighth notes</u> –

♩ = 90-105

Ascending   Descending

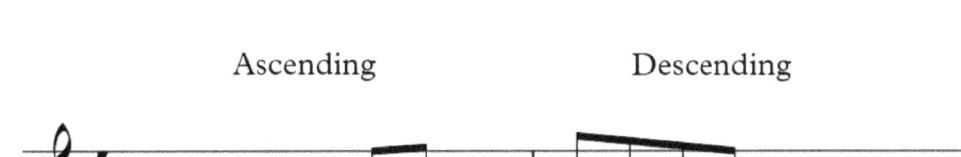

Track 5

Right hand fingering shown

The problem with practicing the above scale as written is that the quarter note at the end of each measure creates a pause in the rhythmical flow. This is because there are only six notes in this scale (seven if you include the octave). One way to avoid this is to add another eighth note at the end of each measure. This gives you an un-interrupted flow of eighth notes that creates a nice swing feel. A suitable way to do this is to repeat the note just before the quarter note. Practice the following exercise until you achieve a nice consistent rhythmical flow –

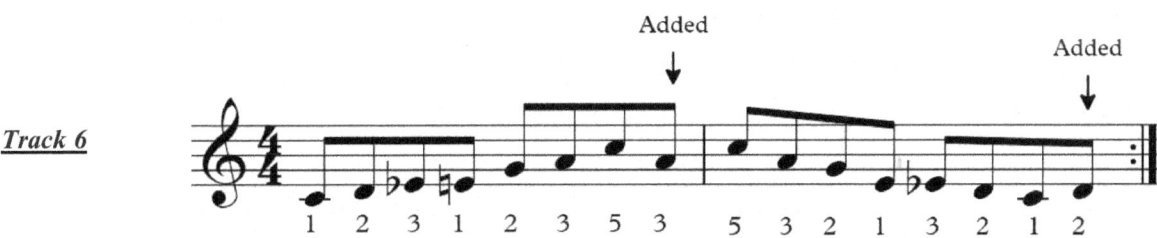

Track 6

Right hand fingering shown

CHAPTER FOUR - COMBING SCALES AND COMP CHORDS

COMBINING THE MAJOR BLUES SCALE AND LEFT HAND COMPING CHORDS

A good way to practice any scale is by adding in left hand comp chords as you play the scale with your right hand. The chords function somewhat like a clock to help sync the right and left hands. To start, play a basic root-seven shell chord in the left hand while playing the C major blues scale with the right hand. If this is new for you then the right hand fingering transition at the bar line may seem tricky at first. <u>Keep the tempo slow as indicated</u>. Remember to swing the eighth notes –

♩ = 90-105

Ascending

Track 7

Descending

Track 8

Ascending   Descending

Track 9

Here, the right hand still plays the C major blues scale, but changes to triplets. Since you are playing triplets, slow the tempo down as indicated –

♩ = 75-85

Track 10

Track 11

ADDING RHYTHMICAL VARIATION IN THE LEFT HAND

Back on pages twelve and thirteen, we looked at some different rhythms to use for the left hand comp chords. Here we will use these rhythms in the left hand while the right hand plays the major blues scale. Notice that the rootless comping chords are utilized rather than the shell chords. You should repeat each exercise without stopping until a smooth rhythmical flow is achieved. Use a metronome set to the tempo indicated. Each exercise is shown more than once offering different articulation markings. A dot (.) above a chord means that chord is to be played short (no sustain). Notice that the right hand scale is played an octave higher so as to not collide with the left hand comp chord –

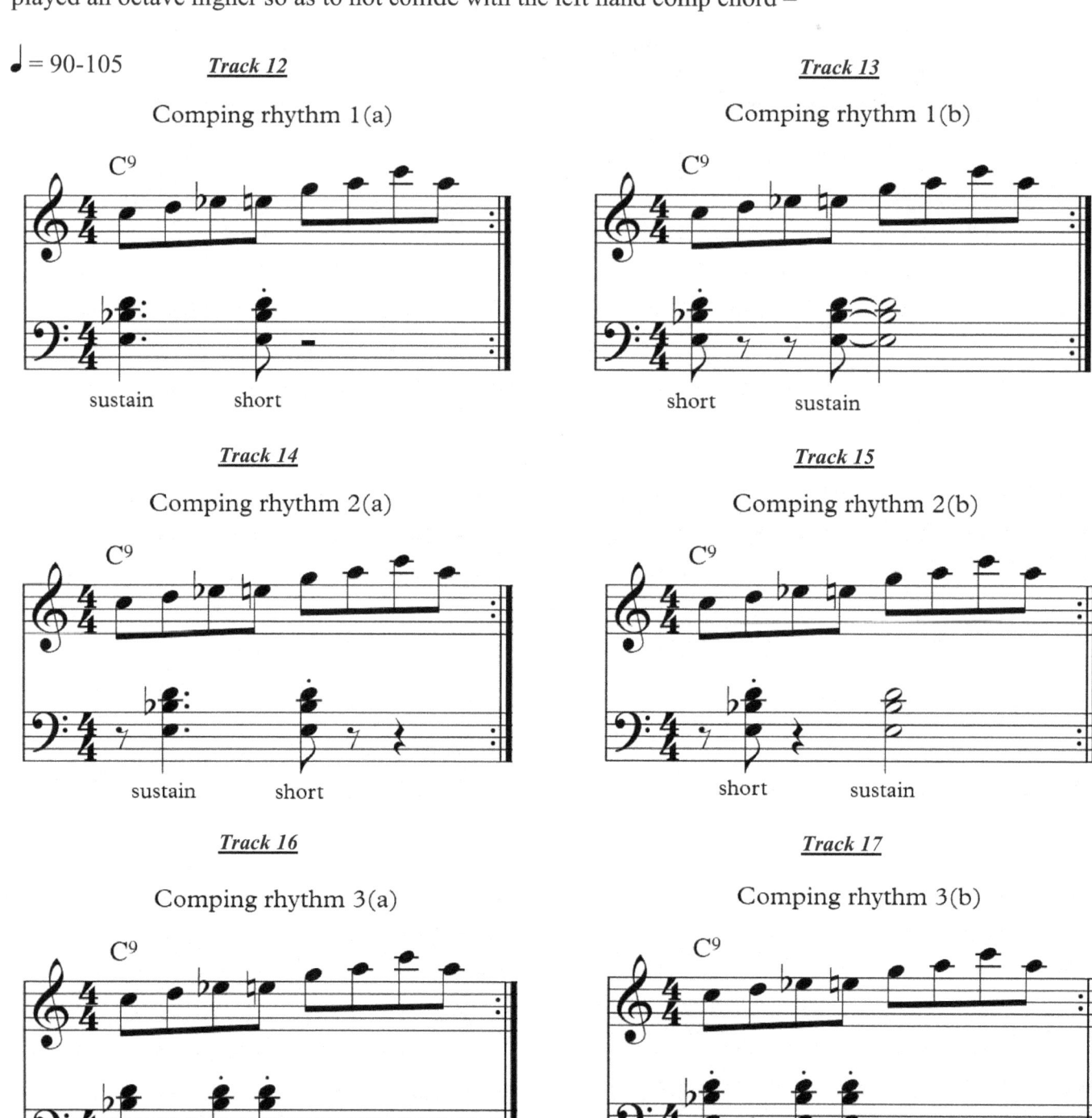

Track 18
Comping rhythm 3(c)

COMP CHORDS WITH RIGHT HAND TRIPLETS

In the following three exercises the right hand still uses the major blues scale but changes to triplets. The left hand comp chord rhythms have not changed but must now play in step with the triplets played in the right hand. Because triplets are used, **slow the tempo down as indicated on the tempo marking**. <u>This section can be tricky so keep the tempo slow.</u> If need be, return to this page at a later time –

♩ = 75-85

Track 19
Comping rhythm 1

Track 20
Comping rhythm 2

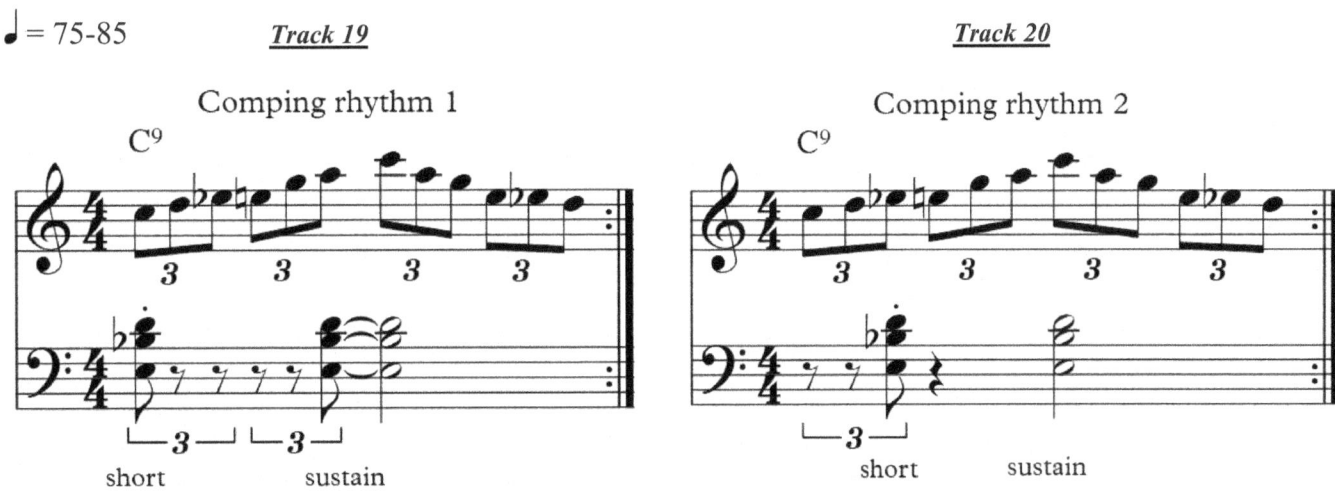

Track 21
Comping rhythm 3

<u>More optional practice ideas</u>

1. Go through the last three exercises again reversing the left hand articulations i.e. make the short chords long and the long chords short.

2. Go back through comping rhythms 1a – 3c with the right hand scale descending.

CHAPTER FIVE - IMPROVISING BASICS

IMPROVISING OVER THE I⁷, IV⁷, AND V⁷ CHORDS

Any of the notes from the major blues scale can be used to play over any of the three chords we are using (I⁷, IV⁷, and V⁷). There is only one exception to this. <u>When playing the IV⁷ chord, the major third must not be played.</u> That note is E if you are playing in the key of C. The reason is self-evident when you hear them played together. Try this test – play an F⁷ block chord in your left hand (F, A, C, E♭) while at the same time playing the E solo note in your right hand. <u>The result is a very dissonant sound.</u>

Therefore:

When playing the IV⁷ chord avoid using the major third as a solo or melody note.

CREATE A RIFF IN THREE STEPS:

A blues can be created by first creating one or more riffs and then placing these riffs in a twelve bar progression. <u>A riff is simply a small group of notes that gets repeated</u> –

1. Pick a small group of notes. Since we want to play a blues solo in C we will pick three to five <u>adjacent notes</u> from the C major blues scale. This is called a <u>scale fragment</u>.
2. Choose a rhythmical pattern to play these notes. This pattern can be as short as one beat or it can be several measure's in length.
3. Choose an order to play these notes in.

Now let's put the above formula to work to create a simple twelve bar blues in the key of C:

<u>Step one</u> - we choose a fragment from the C major blues scale. I am going to choose three adjacent scale notes G, A, and C:

<u>Step two</u> - I have chosen this rhythmic pattern that is one measure long:

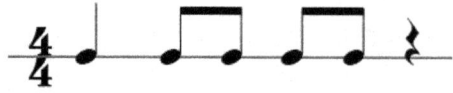

Step three - I have chosen the following order to play the notes in:

Now, let's put this riff into a twelve bar blues. Because this riff will be played over the IV⁷ chord, it does not contain the major third (avoid note) –

Track 22

CHANGING THE ORDER OF THE NOTES

Here is the same twelve bar blues with the notes of the riff played in a different order. Notice that the scale fragment and rhythmic pattern have not changed. **This is a very important point - once you have created a simple riff, that riff can easily be modified by changing the order of the notes –**

<u>Track 23</u>

> **Optional** - can you come up with some more ways to play the above riff? Just change the order of the notes. Don't change the scale fragment or rhythmic pattern yet.

Here we create a new blues from scratch using three new riffs:

1. <u>Choose a scale fragment</u>

2. <u>Choose the rhythmic patterns</u>   3. <u>Choose the note orders</u>

Riff 1

Riff 2

Riff 3

Now let's create a blues with these new riffs. Notice that because both riff #2 and riff #3 get played over the IV⁷ chord that neither of these riffs contains a major third (avoid note) –

Track 24

Here is another twelve bar blues. This time, you choose the notes of the melody using the same rhythmic patterns provided on the top line. Choose notes (or a fragment) from the C major blues scale. Experiment with one riff at a time. Once you get something you like pencil in your note choices directly below the rhythmic pattern using the blank staff provided. Measure twelve uses a couple of notes that are not part of the C major blues scale. These notes will be discussed in chapter eleven (the minor blues scale) –

Track 25

♩ = 120

CHAPTER 6 - RIFF PLACEMENT

Interesting melodies (and solos) can be created when using more than one type of riff and then placing these riffs at specific points within the progression. Placed properly, these riffs create a language that resembles someone talking or in some cases, two people having a conversation. When we write sentences, we use commas and periods to separate different ideas into groups. Similarly, when we speak, these commas and periods come across as pauses and stops. In the first exercise below this stop (or pause) happens during the one measure of rest that occurs between riffs. This pausing and stopping is one of the things you want to be listening for when playing through the simple examples that follow. The first exercise is shown with a left hand accompaniment using 1/7 chord shells. **The remainder of the examples in this chapter only show the right hand melody but I would recommend adding in left hand shell chords in like manner for all of these examples.** Be aware that the <u>riff numbers</u> are not always consistent from example-to-example. For instance – <u>riff 1</u> in the first example is not the same <u>riff 1</u> as in the second example. Keep the tempo at about 110. **As always, any riff played over the IV^7 chord will not have a major third (avoid note) in it.**

ONE RIFF PLACEMENT *Track 26*

Here is the same simple riff placement used on page 21. Only one riff is used. Because this riff gets played over the IV^7 chord, the major third (E) has not be used as one of the notes of the riff –

TWO RIFF PLACEMENT

In this example, a riff #2 is added to measure five –

Track 27

Here, a riff #2 is added to measures nine and ten instead –

Track 28

THREE RIFF PLACEMENT

In this example, three different riffs are used. Because both Riff #2 and riff #3 get played over the IV^7 chord, neither of these riffs contain a major third –

Track 29

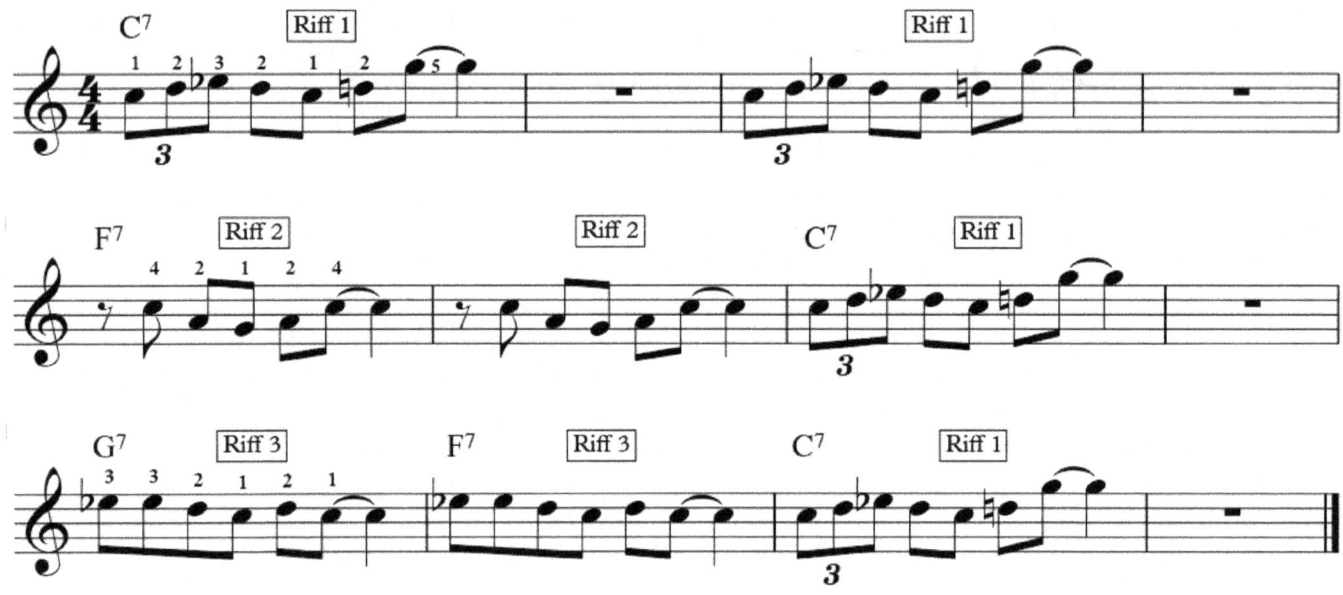

Here is another way of placing three different riffs into a twelve bar blues. Listen for the <u>call and response</u> happening in bars one and three. Bar one being the call - and bar three being the response. It sounds like two people having a conversation. This same <u>call and response</u> is repeated in bars five and seven –

Track 30

FOUR RIFF PLACEMENT

This riff placement is simular to the last one but an extra riff #4 is added in measure ten –

Track 31

FIVE RIFF PLACEMENT

Track 32

SIX RIFF PLACEMENT

In this example, six different riffs are used. The rhythmical pattern is the same for each riff. Only the notes (pitch) change –

Track 33

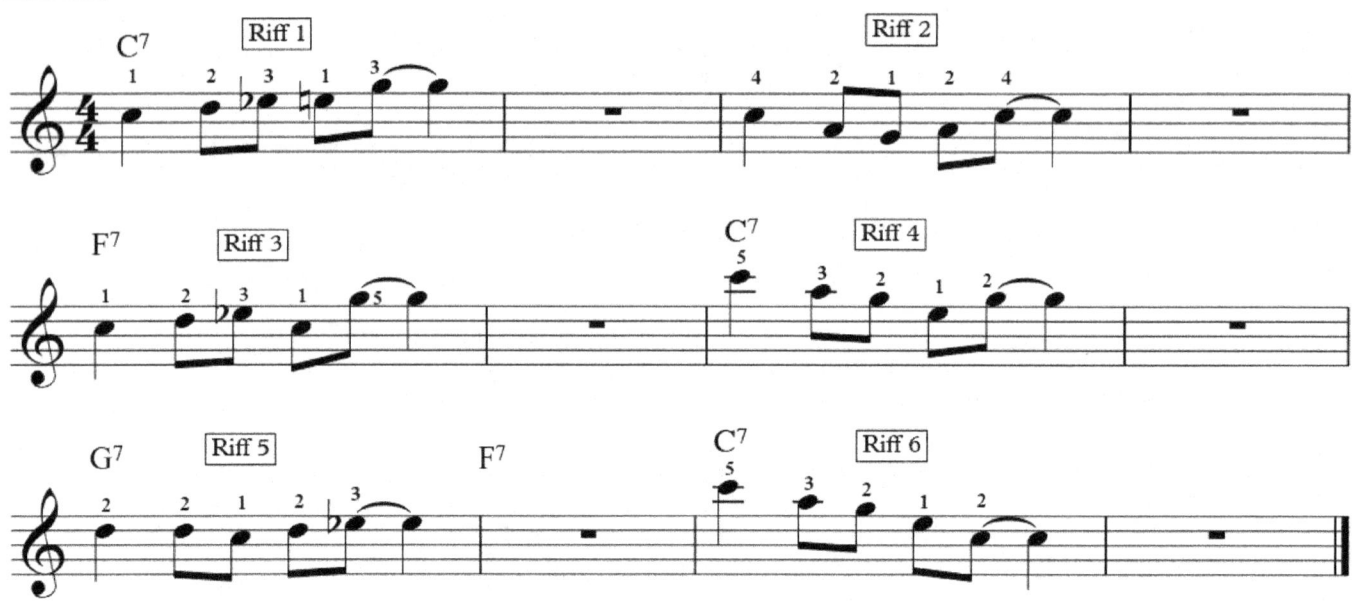

PLACEMENT OF A TWO BAR RIFF

In this last example, only one two bar riff is used. Because the riff gets played over the IV⁷ chord, it does not contain a major third –

Track 34

These riff replacement examples are not exhaustive. Riffs can be placed in many other ways.

CHAPTER 7 - CREATING A BLUES

In chapter five and six we explored creating a blues by first creating some riffs and then placing these riffs into the twelve bar form. In this chapter we explore writing your own twelve bar blues using riffs that you create. In the appendix I have provided two pages of single bar rhythmic patterns to use for creating riffs. To create a two bar riff simply combine any two single bar patterns. The appendix also has a twelve bar composition template you can use for writing out your compositions. This template includes an extra line on top of the staff for writing in the rhythmic patterns. **The first three steps that follow are simply a review on how to create a riff (as explained in previous chapters). Steps four and five deal with riff placement and left hand accompaniment.**

Here are five steps to creating a blues –

1. **Choose between one and three rhythmic patterns from the appendix. You can start with just one pattern (one riff) if you are new to this.**

2. **Pick two to five adjacent notes from the C major blues scale (scale fragment). Again, if your new to this I would suggest starting with only two notes.**

3. **Using the notes from the scale fragment, assign notes (pitches) to each rhythmic pattern. Write these new riffs down in a note book or elsewhere.** It's a good idea to keep a copy of all your riffs.

4. **Using the sheet provided in the appendix (or staff paper), place your riffs with-in the twelve bar form. If you need help in where to place the riffs go back and review the riff placement examples in chapter six. Again, it's ok to use only one riff using the one riff placement idea (a one measure riff – followed by a measure of rest).**

5. **Add a left hand accompaniment -** once you have your right hand worked out its time to add a left-hand accompaniment. To get started, I suggest using the left hand accompaniment that you used back on the top of page 12. Go back and review that page first and then try using that accompaniment along with the right hand part you just wrote. **This simple left hand comping rhythm will allow you to focus more on the right hand.** You can experiment with different comping rhythms later. Now, play through the tune you have created several times (including the left hand accompaniment) until you can play it without looking at the music. As always, it's a good idea to play with a metronome or a rhythm machine set to a slow tempo swing beat.

Once you have created a twelve bar blues, don't be afraid to change things around a bit. If you like what you have, great! If not, then make some changes. Don't be afraid to experiment. I suggest writing only a couple of songs for now. The next several chapters in the book will give you more idea's for creating a blues. Then you can return to this section.

CHAPTER 8 – MORE TWELVE BAR EXAMPLES

Hopefully, you should now have at least some idea of how to create your own twelve bar blues from scratch. The book now takes a turn and focuses on playing through various twelve bar blues tunes. One of the ways you learn how to write a blues (or create a solo line) is by listening to many examples. That is the purpose of the example tunes in this book. I also suggest listening to a lot of blues and jazz music (live or recorded). I want to point out that the formulaic method for creating a blues presented up to this point (riff creation and placement) is not adhered to 100% of the time in the following examples. Although, starting with a rhythm is the way I usually write melodies I also use my ear and adjust the sound to my liking. The tunes in this book are a mix of <u>creating and placing riffs</u> combined with <u>using my ear</u> to change the melody as I hear it.

The melodies in this chapter were all created using the six note major blues scale. No other notes are utilized. As always, the third has been avoided when playing over the IV^7 chord. For your convenience, I have provided right hand fingerings. Occasionally, you will notice <u>alternative fingerings</u> shown just below the treble staff (in parenthesis). Since no two hands are the same these fingerings may or may not work for you. If they help, use them! As you work through the tune, <u>I suggest penciling in your preferred fingerings</u>. **All the tunes in this book should be played with a swing feel like mentioned back on page seven.**

> **All the melodies in this chapter were created using the six note major blues scale. No other notes are utilized.**
> **All the tunes in this book should be played with a swing feel like mentioned back on page seven.**

Track 35

Tune 1

In this first exercise, some new left hand chords are being used not previously mentioned in this book. They are simple seventh chords with no added extension notes. I suggest going through the left hand by itself a few times until you have it down. Then add the right hand. <u>As with all the tunes in this book, don't forget to swing the eight notes.</u>

Track 36

Tune 2

Here is the same exercise again using <u>rootless comping chord sequence 'A'</u> in the left hand along with a different chord rhythm -

Track 37

Tune 3

Here we uses root/7 shells in the left hand -

Track 38 # Tune 4

Measure two of this tune uses a slip note. Slip notes are when the finger <u>slips-off</u> of a raised key (black key) and lands on a lower key (white key). In this case, E♭ slips onto E natural. If you see the piano fingering in this book using the same finger number twice in a row, more often than not, it is a slip note. An alternate non-slip note fingering is provided below the treble staff –

Four new chords for a new chord sequence are introduced here. This new chord sequence will be used for numerous tunes through the remainder of this book –

Tune 5

Track 39

Since this is a new chord sequence I suggest going through the left hand chords by themselves first. Once you have the left hand down add the right hand. Several slip notes are noted here but have an optional non-slip note fingering shown below the treble staff (in parenthesis) –

GRACE NOTES AND DOUBLE CHROMATICS

A grace note is an extra note placed in front of the primary note. Grace notes add texture and have the effect of thickening the primary note. They generally approach the primary note from below but can also approach it from above. Double chromatics are simular but have two notes in front of the primary note. Grace notes generally use two separate fingers (as shown below) however, they can also be played like a slip note if the grace note is on a raised black key and the primary note is on a lower white key –

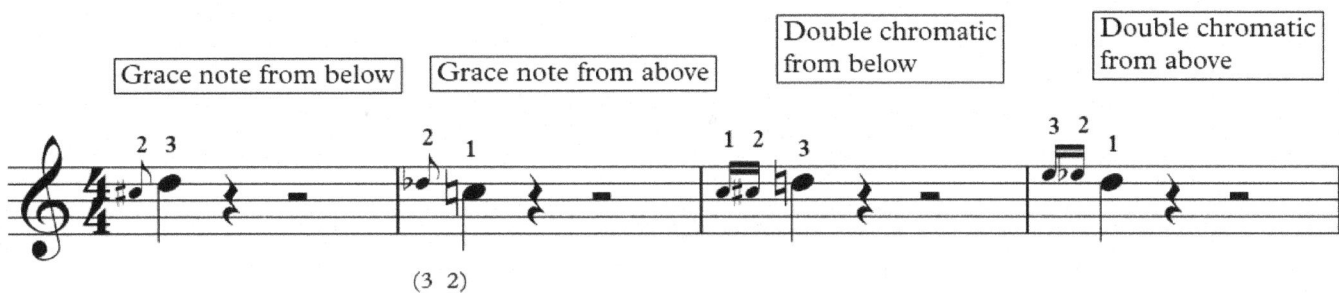

Track 40

Tune 6

Several grace notes have been added in the right hand melody. Grace notes that can be played like a slip note (that start on a raised black key) are shown with an arrow. Non slip note fingerings are also provided –

Tune 7

Track 42

Tune 8

Track 43

Tune 9

Track 44

Tune 10

Pay special attention to the right and left hand note durrations (short-vs-long) –

Track 45

Tune 11

The <u>left hand half note chords</u> in this tune tend to sound like a train going down the tracks. Play them as written but then try shortening the half notes to quarter notes and see how that sounds (keep all other non-half note chords as written) –

Track 46

Tune 12

Guide tones are used in the left hand up until measure nine. Then they change to root/seven chord shells (see pages 9 and 10) –

DOUBLE-STOPS

Double-stop is a term used to describe placing an extra note <u>above</u> an existing melody note. You notice I said **above the melody.** This is an important distinction when compared to say adding harmonic thirds to a melody. Harmonic thirds generally get placed **below the melody line** and not above it. Acceptable notes to add as double-stops are as follows –

<u>If you are using the major blues scale you have three possible choices</u>: you can place the root, 5th, or 6th above the melody line. In the key of C that is C, G or A. I am referring to the root, 5th and 6th of the <u>blues scale</u> and not necessarily the root, 5th, or 6th of the chord you are currently playing. I would add that using the 6th as a double-stop sounds especially good when playing over the IV^7 chord.

<u>If you are using the minor blues scale (coming up in chapter 11)</u>: you can place the root or 5th above the melody line. In the key of C those notes are C (root) and G (5th).

> **Examples of using double-stops follow on the next few pages.**

Track 47

Tune 13

This is the same exercise you played at the beginning of this chapter (tune 1) but with **some added double-stops** –

Track 48

Tune 14

This tune is shown with all of the double-stops removed. The tune is then repeated on the next page with double-stops added –

Track 49

Tune 15

Same as the last tune but **with added double-stops** –

> **OPTIONAL** – If you have an interest in creating blues songs this would be a good time to go back to chapter seven and try your hand at writing a couple more tunes. Hopefully, after going through this last chapter you now have some more idea's in your tool box for writing a twelve bar blues. After you have created your basic blues try spicing it up by adding some double-stops and/or grace notes.
>
> As you continue on with this book you will hopefully come up with more ways to be creative (including adding harmony to your melody as explained in chapter thirteen). The way you learn to write tunes is by doing so. <u>I can't stress that enough</u>! I hope this book inspires you to go to the next level in learning to write music.

CHAPTER 9 - PLAYING WITH BACKING TRACKS

There is of course some differences in writing a melody and trying to improvise. One of the misconceptions about improvising however, is that you must always create the solo spontaneously (in the moment). <u>This is only true some of the times.</u> **The majority of soloists start there solo with licks that they already know.** You can do the same using riffs that you have created back in chapter seven (or any of the riffs used in chapter six). **Here is a way to get started at improvising –**

Find a twelve bar blues track in the key of C that doesn't have too fast a tempo (110 is good). Blues tracks in different keys and tempo's can be found on the internet. They can also be purchased. Make sure the tracks you choose are using the same simple twelve bar chord progression that is being utilized in this book (see page #7). Other twelve bar blues chord progressions do exist. However, that may require more specific knowledge on what to do in those cases. Best off to start out simple. Also, keep in mind that some blues tracks will use a <u>quick four</u> and some will not (see page #8). If the track is using a quick four then you will have to change the chord on that measure accordingly. If you are also soloing over that measure, you will have to avoid the major third (avoid note) from any licks you use over that measure. Now that you have some tracks to play lets get started –

1. Start the track and play along with it using the <u>one riff placement</u> shown on page 26. **Just play the right hand melody as written. The left hand can remain idol for now.** Play through the twelve bar blues in this fashion several times until you feel comfortable with it.

2. Now move on to the <u>two riff placement</u> on page 27. Do the same thing. Just play the right hand melody as written along with the track (still no left hand chords yet).

3. Continue through the rest of the chapter in like manner – playing each exercise as written.

ADDING THE LEFT HAND ACCOMPANIMENT

4. Now go back to the <u>one riff placement</u> (page 26). Start the track and **play both hands as written.** Again, play through the track as many times as needed to achieve a nice flow and with a minimal amount of mistakes.

5. Continue back through the rest of the chapter in like manner **adding in the left hand**.

   Hopefully by now you are having some real fun doing this.

6. **Now try playing one of the tunes you wrote in chapter seven along with the track!!** This can be a tune with just one riff or with many riffs. Its up to you. Again, I suggest starting with the right hand by itself. Once you have the right hand down, add the left hand chords. Another thing you can experiment with is using some different left hand comping rhythms (see pages 18 and 19).

The process I am presenting here is just a door way to help you begin to improvise. To develop your own style you must experiment with different riffs and riff placements. As you become more comfortable playing with the tracks experiment a little by changing some things around a bit. How about changing one note of one of the riffs? How about changing two notes? How about creating some two bar riffs and use those? Experimentation is an important key!

CHAPTER 10 - OTHER NOTES TO USE WITH THE MAJOR BLUES SCALE

The six note major blues scale can be enhanced by periodically <u>adding</u> other notes to it. If used only occasionally, these new notes give a nice diversion of sound to the melody or solo.

ADDING THE ♭7 TO THE MAJOR BLUES SCALE

The ♭7 in the key of C is B♭ –

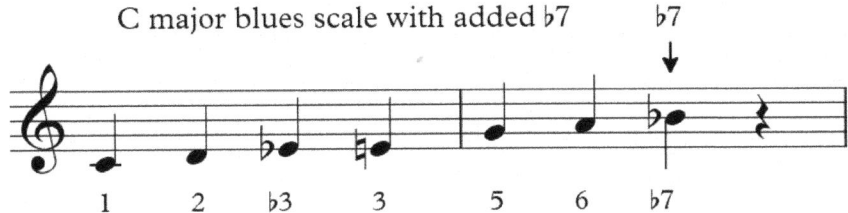

<u>The ♭7 is a very friendly note to add to the major blues scale.</u> You can generally use it and it sounds good. This is not always the case when attempting to add an extra tone to this scale. Sometimes more caution needs to be exercized or you can end up doing more harm than good. Your ear, of course, will have the final say.

> An example of using the added ♭7 follows on the next page.

Tune 16

Track 50

Adding the ♭7 to the major blues scale – the arrows show the location of the ♭7. The left hand uses guide tones through-out. Be careful at measure eleven as the left and right hands become very close to coliding –

ADDING THE ♭6 TO THE MAJOR BLUES SCALE

Another note that can be periodically added to the major blues scale is the ♭6 (A♭ in the key of C). However, this note is very unforgiving (sounds awful) unless used as a <u>passing tone</u> or a <u>half-step approach tone</u>. Here is the C major blues scale with the added ♭6 –

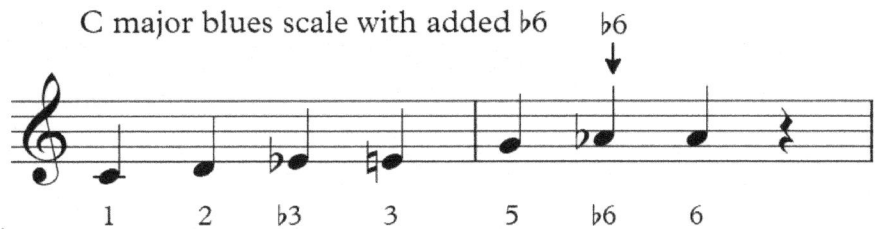

THE ♭6 AS A PASSING TONE

A passing tone is a note that is not part of the scale and <u>passes</u> quickly between two main scale tones. The ♭6 is not a note from the major blues scale but sits between two main scale tones. Namely, the 5th and the 6th. In the following example, the ♭6 is called a <u>chromatic passing tone</u> because it is a half-step away from both the 5th and the 6th. Here are two examples of the ♭6 being used as a chromatic passing tone –

THE ♭6 AS A HALF STEP APPROACH TONE

A half step approach tone is a note that precedes a main scale tone by a half step. It is, like the passing tone, a fairly quick note (you don't camp-out on it for long). Here are two examples of the ♭6 being used as a half step approach tone. In the first instance the 6th is approached from below by the ♭6. In the second instance the 5th is approached from above by the ♭6 –

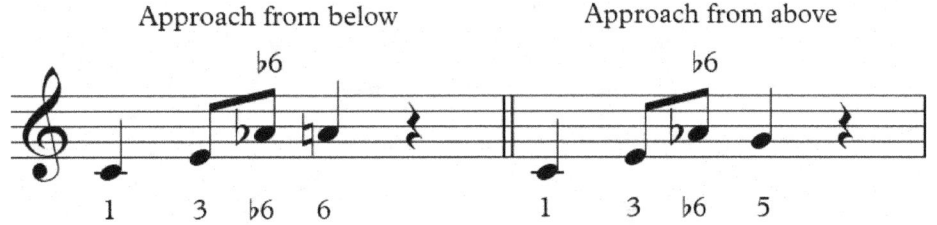

Track 51 **Tune 17**

Adding the ♭6 to the major blues scale – the arrows show the location of the ♭6. In measures three and six, the ♭6 is used as a passing tone. In all other instances it is use as a half step approach to the the 6th –

Track 52

Tune 18

In this example, the ♭6 is used as a passing tone only. The left hand accompaniment uses a combination of seventh chords and 1/7 chord shells. Several slip notes are used as indicated by the top fingerings (two of the same note numbers in a row generally indicate slip note). The non-slip note fingerings are shown below the treble staff in parenthesis. This tune should be played <u>slower</u> as indicated by the tempo marking –

Track 53

Tune 19

Here again we add a ♭6 to the major blues scale (denoted with arrow). This time with added double-stops –

Track 54

Tune 20

Adding the 11th or #11 to the major blues scale – here is a tune with an added 11th. Although, the #11 is not exampled here, it can also be utilized –

Track 55

Tune 21

Adding both the ♭6 and ♭7 to the major blues scale – all instances of the ♭6 are passing tones. The fingerings on top are slip-note fingerings while the alternate fingerings written below (in parenthesis) are non-slip note fingerings –

CHAPTER 11 - THE MINOR BLUES SCALE

The minor blues scale is derived from the minor pentatonic scale. The minor pentatonic scale is derived from the minor scale. The numbers below the staff refer to the scale degree:

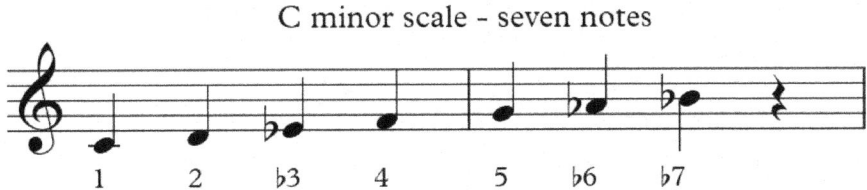

Omit the 2nd and the b6th to get the minor pentatonic scale:

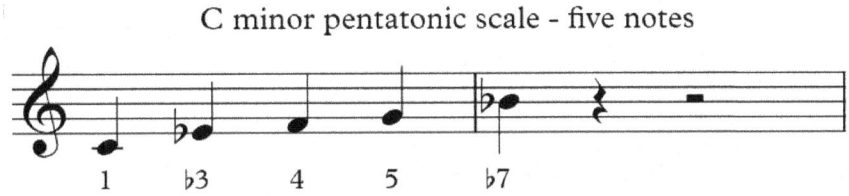

And finally, add the b5 to obtain the minor blues scale:

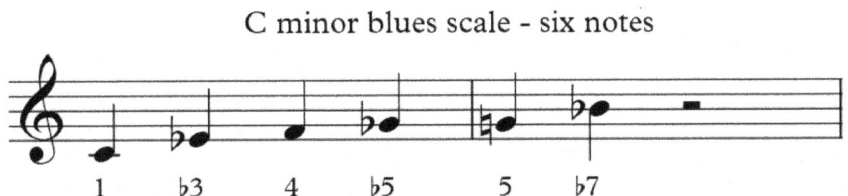

RELATIVE MAJOR AND MINOR BLUES SCALES

Back in chapter one I mentioned that every major scale has a relative minor scale and conversely, every minor scale has a relative major scale. The same relationship exists between a major and minor blues scale. As an example, to find the relative minor blues scale of the C major blues scale, count down three half steps from the tonic (C) and you arrive at 'A'. Therefore, the A minor blues scale is the relative minor of the C major blues scale. The opposite is also true – the C major blues scale is the relative major of the 'A' minor blues scale. That means if you know any one blues scale in any key (major or minor) you automatically know its relative scale. The notes of both scales are the same. The only difference is the note you start on.

Practice the minor blues scale as shown below. Just like the major blues scale, it only has six notes so it lends itself to practicing within the triplet realm very well (six notes to form two triplets). Pay attention to the tempo marking. The numbers below the staff give the <u>right hand fingering</u>:

♩ = 75-85

Minor blues scale – one octave

Track 56

Right hand fingering shown

Now practice the two octave version of the same scale:

Track 57

Minor blues scale – two octaves

Right hand fingering shown

IMPROVISING OVER THE I⁷, IV⁷, AND V⁷ CHORDS

Any of the notes from the minor blues scale can be used to play over any of the three chords we are using (I^7, IV^7, and V^7). Unlike the major blues scale, **there are no avoid notes**.

> **All the melodies in this chapter were created using the six note minor blues scale. No other notes are utilized.**

Track 58   **Tune 22**

Here is tune #2 again (page 34) but adapted to the C minor blues scale –

Track 59

Tune 23

Track 60

Tune 24

Track 61

Tune 25

Here we alternate between two bars of melody followed by two bars of two hand chords. A $G^{7\,(\flat 13)}$ chord is used in measure nine –

Track 62

Tune 26

Here again is two measures of right hand melody followed by two measures of two hand chords –

Track 63

Tune 27

Measures 2, 4, 6, and 12 use added chord motion in the left hand. In each case the chord momentarily drops a half-step and then returns back up a half-step to the original chord –

Track 64

Tune 28

This tune is repeated again on the next page with double-stops added –

Tune 29

Track 65

Here is the same tune again with double-stops added. As mentioned earlier, acceptable double-stop notes to add to the minor blues scale are the root and the 5th (see page 47) –

Track 66

Tune 30

This is a slower tempo blues as indicated by the tempo marking. **The double-stops use both roots and 5ths as the upper added note** –

CHAPTER 12 - OTHER NOTES TO USE WITH THE MINOR BLUES SCALE

Optional – If you have the interest, this would be a good time to go back to chapter seven and write a couple of twelve bar tunes using the minor blues scale. Then return to this chapter.

The six note minor blues scale can be enhanced by periodically using some other notes along with it. If used only occasionally, these new notes give a nice diversion of sound to the melody or solo. I must add (with emphasis) that these added tones should be used as suggested or you may do more harm than good. There are of course some acceptions to this but I suggest keeping it simple for now. Here is a chart summarizing these added tones along with how to use them –

TONE	USAGE
Major 7th	Chromatic passing tone between the ♭7 and root. It can be ascending or descending.
	Half-step approach tone <u>from below to the root</u>.
	Half-step approach tone <u>from above to the ♭7</u>.
3^{erd}	Chromatic passing tone between the ♭3 and the 4th. It can be ascending or descending.
	Half-step approach tone <u>from below to the 4th</u>.
	Half-step approach tone <u>from above to the ♭3</u>.
6th	Passing tone between the 5th and ♭7. It can be ascending or descending.
	Half-step approach tone <u>from below to the ♭7</u>.
9th	Passing tone between the root and ♭3. It can be ascending or descending.
	Half-step approach tone <u>from below to the ♭3</u>.

TONE	**USAGE**
♭9 (♭2)	Half-step approach <u>from above to the root</u>.

A special case arises for the ♭9 when the 9th is also used as an added tone –

♭9 (♭2)	Chromatic passing tone between the root and 9th. It can be ascending or descending.
	Half-step approach <u>from below to the 9th</u>.

> Several tunes follow that illustrate the use of these tones with the minor blues scale.

Track 67

Tune 31

Adding the major 7th to the minor blues scale - the major 7th (B natural) is shown with arrows –

75

Track 68

Tune 32

Here is the same tune again with double-stops added –

ENCLOSURES

An enclosure of a targeted note occurs when that targeted note is first preceded by two other notes. One of these notes being a half-step above – and the other – a half-step below the targeted note. In the following three examples we are using the minor blues scale with an <u>added third</u>. In the first example the third is simply added to the melody line as an <u>ascending chromatic passing tone</u>. In the second example, we enclose the third (targeted note) with two notes. The first note (F) is a half-step above the third. The second note (Eb) is a half-step below the third. The order of the two preceding notes can be reversed as shown in example three –

Example 1

Example 2

Example 3

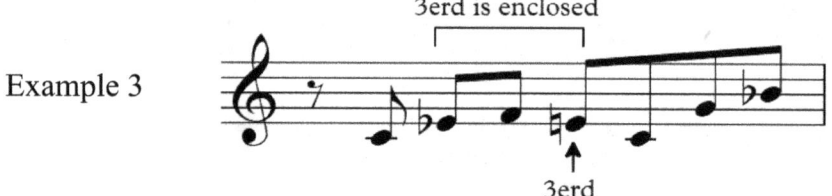

There are many other types of enclosures as well (which goes beyond the scope of this book). If you like the sound I suggest going to the internet or get a music composition book that goes more into depth on the subject.

> The tune on the following page illustrates the use of an enclosure.

Track 69

Tune 33

Adding the major third – the major third (E) is added here as an enclosure in measure one and in measure nine (denoted with arrows) –

Track 70 **Tune 34**

Another example of adding the third – this tune can be a little tricky. You may want to learn the right and left hand parts separately first before playing the hands together. This tune gets played a little faster as noted by the tempo marking –

Track 71

Tune 35

Adding the 6th – the sixth (A) is added sparingly in measure one and measure five (denoted with arrows). Double-stops have also been added –

ADDING THE 9th

The ninth (D) can also be added to the minor blues scale. It can act as a passing tone (ascending or descending) between the root (C) and the b3 (Eb). It can also act as a half-step approach from below to the b3. Although, no example tunes are provide for the 9th some possible uses are provided below –

Track 72

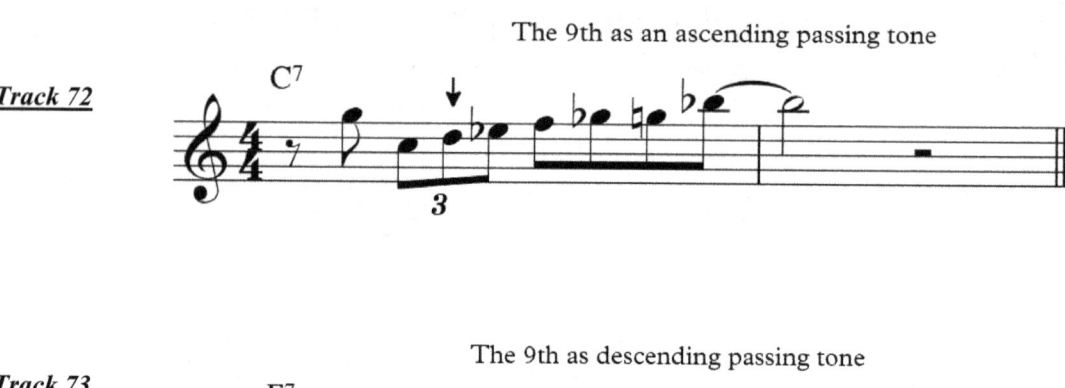

Track 73

Track 74

ADDING THE b9

The b9 (Db) can be used as a half-step approach <u>from above</u> to the root (C). Here are a few possible uses of the b9 –

Track 75

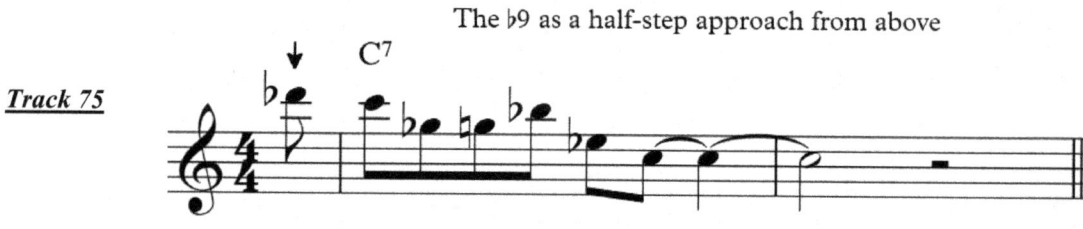

The ♭9 as a half-step approach from above

Track 76

Track 77

The ♭9 as a half-step approach from above

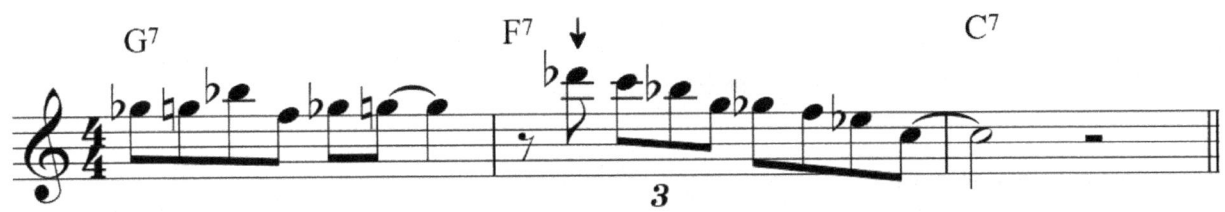

ADDING THE 9th AND THE ♭9 TOGETHER

Several new options open up when you use these two notes together. The ♭9 (D♭) makes a good chromatic passing tone between the root and the 9th. Also, another half-step approach is now possible between the ♭9 and 9th (either direction). Following are a few examples of how you could these tones with the minor blues scale –

The ♭9 as a chromatic passing tone

Track 78

♭9 as a half-step approach from below

Track 79

CHAPTER 13 - ADDING HARMONY TO THE MELODIC LINE

A simple melody can be spiced up with the use of added harmony notes. Unlike double-stops which are added ABOVE the existing melody, harmony notes are added BELOW the existing melody. Harmony notes generally consist of major thirds, minor thirds, and perfect forth intervals. It would be easier if we only had one chord to deal with when adding harmony notes but we have three. The harmony notes we choose may sound good over the I^7 chord but those same note choices may clash with the notes of the IV^7 or V^7 chord. Therefore, three harmonized scales are provided below. One for each of the three chords. **These harmonized scales can be used as a <u>reference guide</u> when you wish to harmonize a blues melody.**

ADDING HARMONY TO THE MAJOR BLUES SCALE

Harmonizing over the I^7 chord – Remember that in each of the following examples the top notes form the major blues scale and the bottom notes are the added harmony. Harmony notes that are not part of the major blues scale are designated by a diamond shaped note head and an arrow. For your convenience, the ♭7 has also been included. –

Harmonizing over the IV^7 chord –

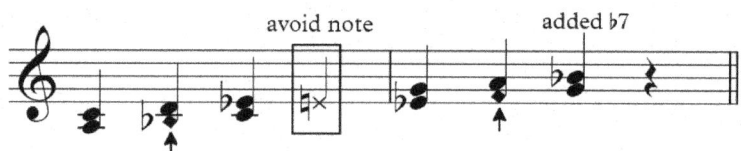

Harmonizing over the V^7 chord –

> The following tunes (#36 and #37) are examples of adding harmony to the major blues scale.

Track 80

Tune 36

Adding harmony to the major blues scale –this is a repeat of tune #20 but with harmony added to the melody –

Track 81

Tune 37

Adding harmony to the major blues scale – here we use both double-stops (denoted with DS) and harmony notes together in the same tune. Vertical note pairs in the right hand not having the DS designator are harmony pairs –

ADDING HARMONY TO THE MINOR BLUES SCALE

Harmonizing over the I⁷ chord. Remember in the following examples that the top notes form the minor blues scale and the bottom notes are the added harmony –

Perfect fourth's

Harmonizing over the IV⁷ and V7 chords – acceptable added harmony notes are the same for both the IV⁷ and V⁷ chords. The arrows and diamond shaped note heads designate harmony notes that are not part of the minor blues scale –

> The following tunes (#38 – #41) are examples of adding harmony to the minor blues scale.

Track 82   **Tune 38**

Adding harmony to the minor blues scale – The trill: a trill is simply a rapid sustained back-and-forth change between two notes. It is written as a long squiggly line (one in measure four and another in measure eight). In this example the two trilled notes are the 5th and b7 which is a very common trill. It takes some practice to get a smooth even sound. The left hand is using 3/7 guide tones and all right hand vertical note pairs are harmonies (no double-stops in this tune) –

Track 83

Tune 39

Adding harmony to the minor blues scale – the left hand Form B chord sequence is used here for the first time (page 11). Because this chord sequence sounds a little too high pitched it doesn't get as much use. Double-stops are designated as DS. All other right hand vertical notes pairs are harmonies –

Track 84 **Tune 40**

Here is the same tune again but with a more difficult syncopated left hand chord rhythm. Your mission (should you decide to accept it) is to start slow. Learning one measure at a time if you need to. We are back to the Form A chord sequence –

Track 85

Tune 41

Adding harmony to the minor blues scale – the 11th (F) is enclosed where indicated. This enclosure is a slightly different type than the one discussed earlier (see page 76). Here the target note is approached from a half step above and then from a <u>whole step below</u> (rather than a half-step below). The 6th is also added to the melody –

CHAPTER 14 - PUTTING IT ALL TOGETHER

I hope the tunes in the previous chapters have <u>trained your ears to recognize the difference between the two scales and to recognize the added tones when they are used</u>. This is a very important aspect of writing a melody or improvising – <u>to be able to put what you hear in your head down on paper or put it down spontaneously as a solo.</u> This of course does not happen overnight.

Another thing I want to mention is the difference in era between these two scales. The major blues scale is reminiscent of earlier blues as far back as the 1920's. It would be a good choice to stay closer to this scale if you want to keep it more traditional. On the other hand, if you like the modern blues sound (and rock) the minor blues scale might be a better choice. In this chapter we will look at ways in which you can use both scales together.

SUMMERY

There are only twelve tones on the piano. Each one of these tones have been discussed in this book in some form or another on its usage. Most of these tones belong to either the major and minor blues scale. There are three exceptions – the ♭9, ♭6, and major 7 do not belong to either scale.

Scale choices you have for improvisation and melody writing –

1. Stick with the traditional major blues scale with some occasional <u>added notes</u>.

2. Stick with the modern sounding minor blues scale with some occasional <u>added notes</u>.

You also have these embellishments to enhance the melody line –

1. Grace notes.

2. Double-stops.

3. Harmony notes.

4. Trills.

Here is a summary of scales and added tones –

<u>Major blues scale:</u>

♭7 - very friendly note. Can be added easily.

♭6 - used as a passing tone or approach tone.

11th and #11.

Minor blues scale:

Major 7 - used as a passing tone or approach tone.

3ʳᵈ - used as a passing tone or approach tone.

6ᵗʰ - used as a passing tone or a half-step approach from below.

9ᵗʰ - used as a passing tone or a half-step approach from below.

♭9 (♭2) - half-step approach from above.

9ᵗʰ and ♭9 together.

COMBINING THE MAJOR AND MINOR BLUES SCALES

There are two ways you can do this –

1. Use the major blues scale exclusively <u>except when playing over the IV⁷ chord</u>. When you are on the IV⁷ chord switch to the minor blues scale. There are no <u>avoid notes</u> to worry about because you are using the minor blues scale which doesn't have a major third in it. This technique has a very nice sound.

2. Switch between the major and minor blues scale at will. <u>Your ear has the final say</u>.

| Following are example tunes for each of these two options. |

Track 86 # Tune 42

The major and minor blues scales together – this tune uses the major blues scale except when on the IV^7 chord where the minor blues scale is used instead –

Switching between the major and minor blues scale at will letting your ear have the final say. Question -

Is the melodic phrase (or riff) I just played from the major or minor blues scale ?

At first this may seem like an irrelevant question. Isn't it a simple matter of which scale I am using? This is true as long as you are not adding any notes that are from the other scale. Let's use the first bar of tune #34 as an example. As shown on the staff below, this riff uses the minor blues scale with an added third. However, this phrase can also be viewed as a major blues scale with an added 11th (shown on the second staff). The added third in the first instance is from the major blues scale (opposite scale) and the added eleventh in the second instant is from the minor scale. When you add a note that is from the other scale you are in effect **combining scales (at least momentarily)**. I guess the point that I am driving at is that **you have already been combining the two scales** when you happen to add a note that is from the other scale. And finally, **there really are no rules about having to stay on any particular scale thruout an entire twelve bar blues.** You can at will change between the two scales at any time. As your ears become more familiar to these scales (and associated added notes) you will find yourself simply using the note and/or notes that sound right to you at that time. **YOUR EARS BECOME THE FINAL SAY**. This is not to negate in any way just sticking with the major or minor blues scale. **Each method has its own unique sound. Use the scale or method that gives you the sound you are after.**

Riff as derived from the C minor blues scale with an added 3erd

Riff as derived from the C major blues scale with an added 11th

Track 87

Tune 43

Using both scales together – This tune utilizes both the major and minor blues scales. It alternates between two bars of the major blues scale (with added ♭7) followed by two bars of the minor blues scale. I am not following any formula here other than what sounded good at the time –

Track 88 **Tune 44**

Using both scales together – this tune starts with the minor blues scale and then changes to the major blues scale (with added ♭6) in bars seven through nine. Measure ten returns to the minor blues scale. Again, no particular formula or method is being used as to which scale I am using. My ear decides measure-by-measure. Double-stops and harmony notes are labeled –

ANOTHER WAY TO CREATE VARIETY IN THE MELODY OR SOLO LINE

CHANGING KEY OVER THE V^7 CHORD – when playing over the V^7 chord in measure nine you can change to the key that is the same as the root of the V^7 chord. **The following measure then returns to the original key.** In the example on the following page, the V^7 chord is G^7. The root of that chord is of course G. So the key signature changes to the key of G (for that measure only). **You can use the G major or minor blues scale during that measure.** This technique can be used over the V^7 chord as you like.

Full analysis of tune #45:

1. The tune starts off using the C minor blues scale with an added 3erd and major 7.

2. At measure nine it changes to the key of G and uses the G major blues scale.

3. Measure ten returns to the key of C and uses the C major blues scale with an added ♭7.

4. The tune finishes off in measures eleven and twelve using the minor blues scale.

All double-stops and harmony notes are labeled.

The grace notes in this tune approach the main tone from above rather than from below. Two fingering options are provided for these grace notes. One uses a grace slip-note fingering and the other does not. You can use the one you prefer.

Track 89

Tune 45

Changing key over the V⁷ chord – see the previous page for a full explanation and analysis –

Track 90 **Tune 46**

Although this tune primarily utilizes the major blues scale (with numerous added tones) I want to draw your attention to measure nine. This measure can be looked at in two ways – as a major blues scale with four added tones or as a minor blues scale with four added tones. Therefore, it is easier to just call it a <u>mixed scale</u>. Notice that the key remains in C at all times. Measure ten returns to the major blues scale –

CHAPTER 15 - SCALE WARM-UP IDEAS

LEFT AND RIGHT HAND WARM-UP EXERCISE

A really good warm up is to play through an entire twelve bar blues using a left hand accompaniment of your choosing while utilizing both the major and minor blues scales in the right hand. In this way, you are practicing both the major and minor blues scales as well as a left hand accompaniment in one exercise. **There are many different ways you can do this**. Since you need to avoid playing the 3erd over the IV⁷ chord you could play the minor blues scale when on those particular measures. Some other options you have are to play the scale with triplets, eighth notes, ascending, descending, or switching between triplets and eighths. For the left hand you could play rootless comping chords, guide tones, 1/7 chord shells, as well as add some rhythmical variations (like on pages 18 and 19). The point here is to come up with your own way of doing it. There really are no rules (isn't that fun)? **The following example is one possible way you can do this:** the major blues scale is used exclusively except when playing over the IV⁷ at which point the minor blues scale is used. The right hand switches between eight notes and triplets. I suggest using the tempo indicated. If you start to fast you may have trouble keeping up when the triplets start –

Track 91

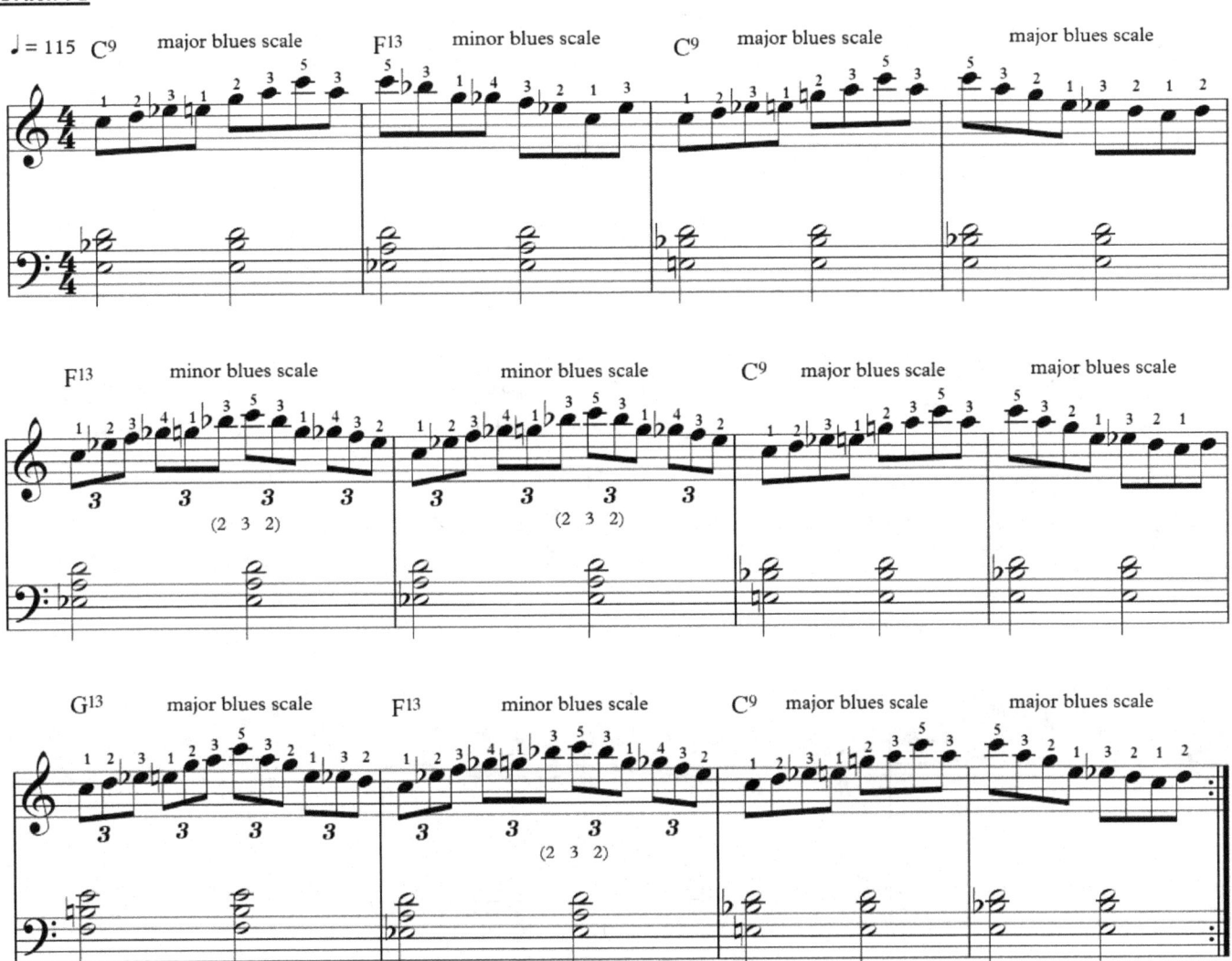

ADDING A RHYTHMICAL COMPONENT TO SCALES

This is a good point to interject another method of creating a riff or improvisation. An entire chapter could be devoted to this topic, however, I want to at least touch upon it. While practicing a scale (any scale) nothing says you must play only eighth notes or only triplets through-out the entire scale. To add interest, try interjecting a new rhythm of your choosing from the rhythm sheets located in the appendix. The idea here is to play the scale using the rhythmic pattern. <u>When you reach the octave of the scale simply turn around and continue back down the scale (or back up the scale if initially descending)</u>. The scale resets to the tonic at the beginning of each new measure (ascending or descending). As always, I encourage you to come up with some of your own ideas. Your imagination is the limit. Here are three rhythmic patterns I have chosen (from the appendix) for the following example exercise –

Track 92

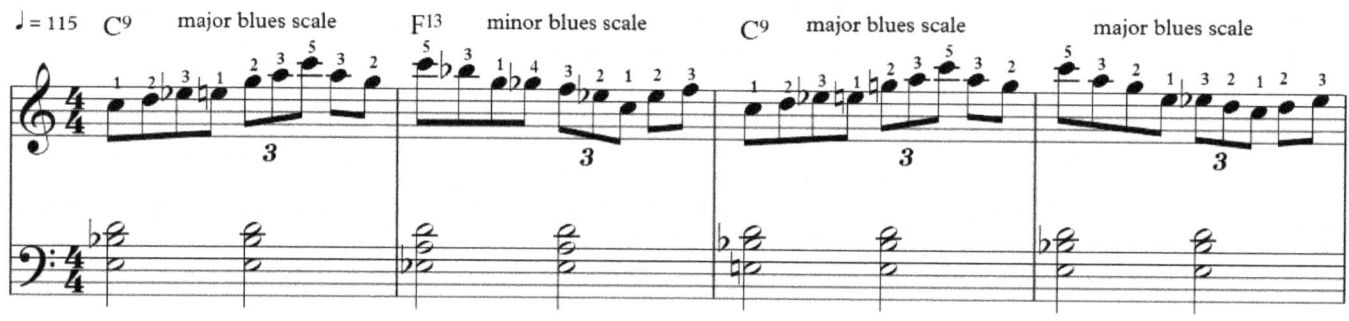

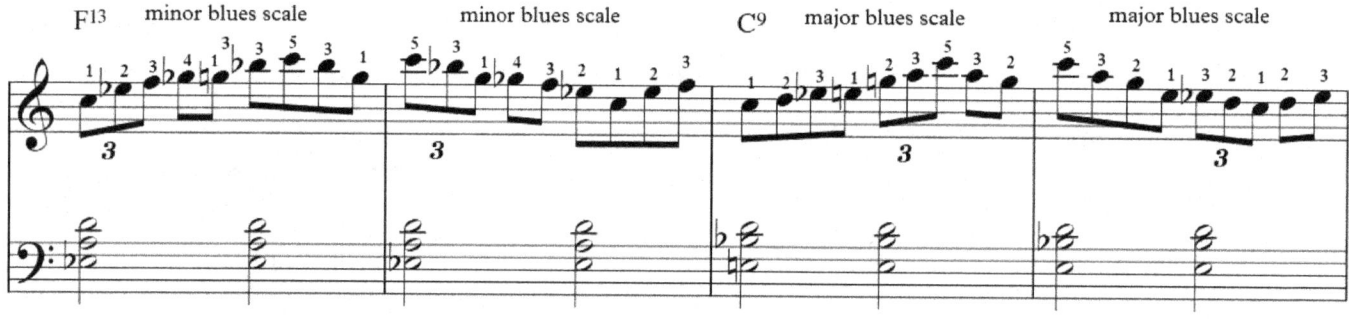

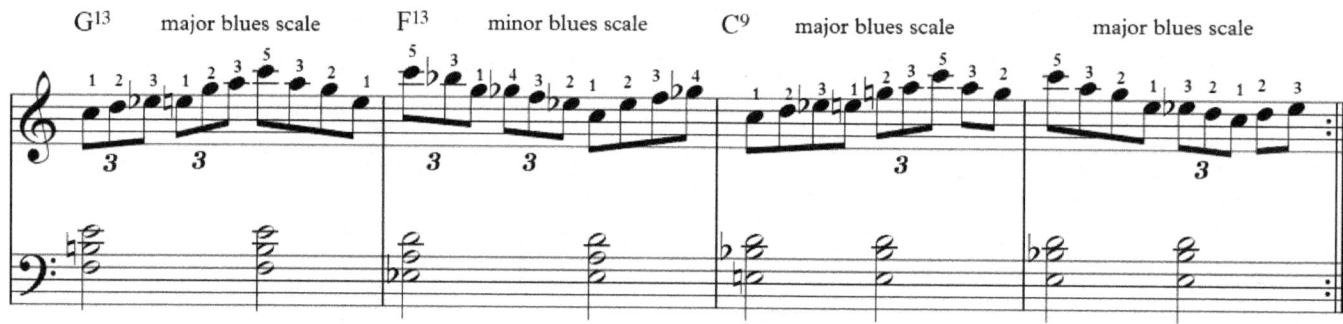

BLANK PAGE

CHAPTER 16 – PLAYING IN OTHER KEYS

Here we will examine playing in three new keys – namely – F, B♭, and G. The tunes provided in each new key are preceded by a scale warm-up sheet. **Go through the warm-up sheet first to familiarize yourself with the notes of the major and minor blues scales of the new key. And then secondly, play through the tunes in that new key.** Separate analysis sheets are provided for each tune as needed. Two detailed reference sheets are also provided for each new key – one for the scales and another for the accompaniment chords.

> **Optional** – in the last chapter I introduced a couple of different ways in which you can practice the right hand scales and the left hand chords together in a twelve bar exercise. If you would like to familiarize yourself a little more with each new key try coming up with your own twelve bar warm-up using some of those ideas. You have both the detailed scale sheets and chord accompaniment sheets at your disposal.

WARM-UP SCALES FOR THE KEY OF F

Back in chapter four (page 17) you added left hand shell chords along with the right hand scale. We are doing the same thing here. Practice the right hand scale by itself at the tempo suggested (no left hand to start with). Once you feel comfortable with the scale try adding in the left hand shell chords –

♩ = 75-85

Major blues scale

Minor blues scale

Tune 47 (in F)

Track 93

See the following page for the analysis of this tune –

Tune 47 analysis

The major blues scale is used up until measure ten where it switches to the minor blues scale. The diamond shaped note heads indicate added notes that are not part of the current scale –

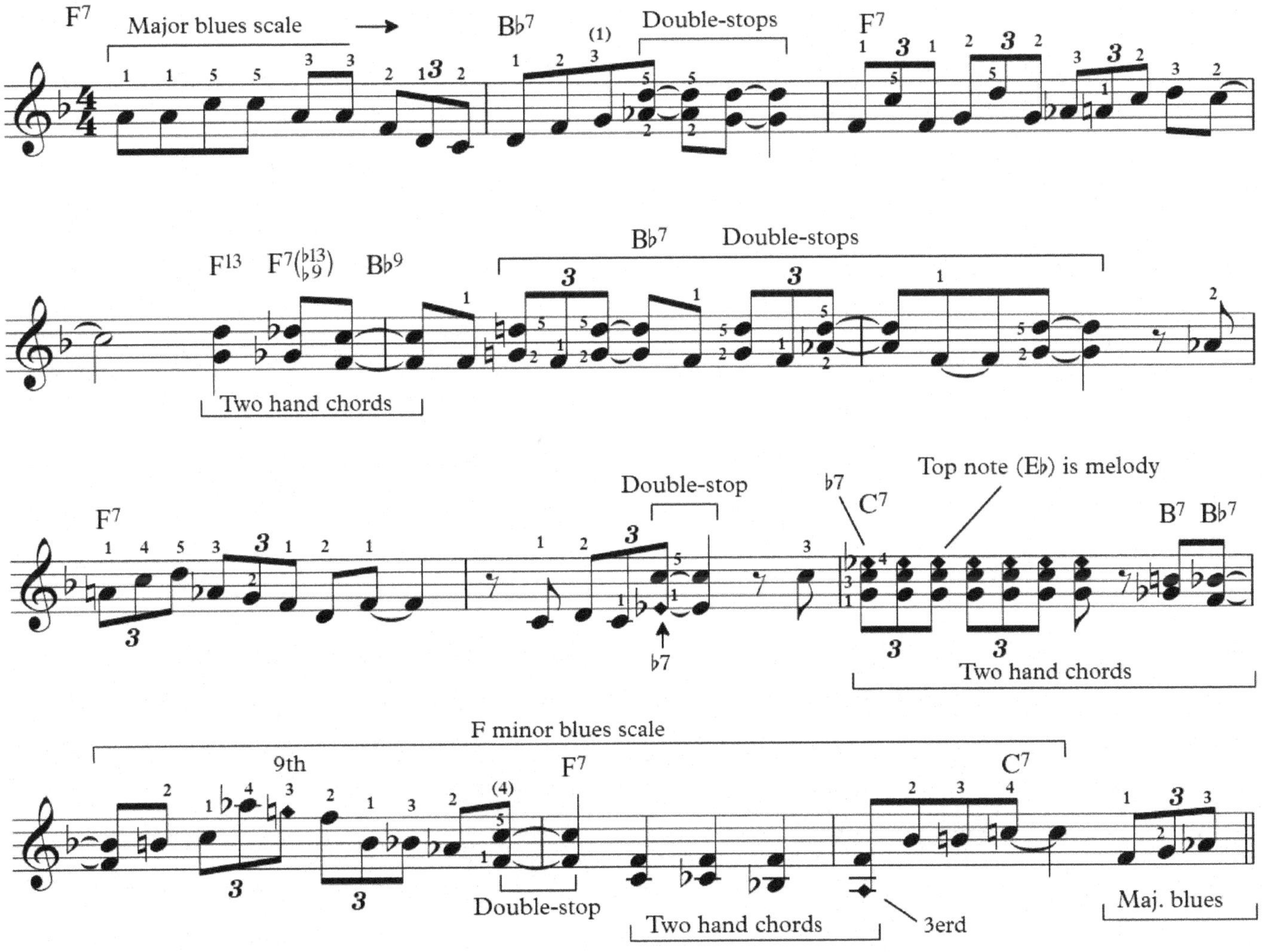

Track 94

Tune 48 (in F)

See the following page for the analysis of this tune –

Tune 48 analysis

This tune has five added tones – the b2, 3erd, b6, 6th and b7. The notes are not labeled but are identified by a small arrow (exception in bar twelve where the b7 is labeled). As a challenge go ahead and pencil in the correct tone names above the arrows. Changes between the major and minor blues scale are labeled with a bracket above the staff -

BLUES SCALES IN F

♩ = 75-85

F major blues scale - six notes

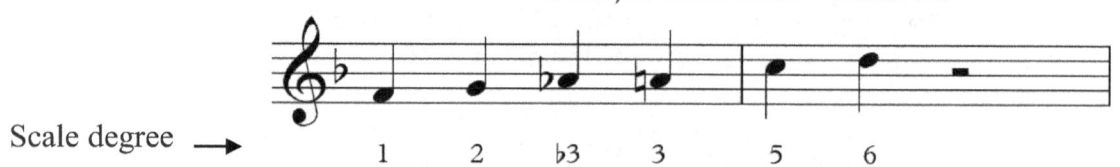

Scale degree → 1   2   ♭3   3   5   6

Major blues scale – one octave

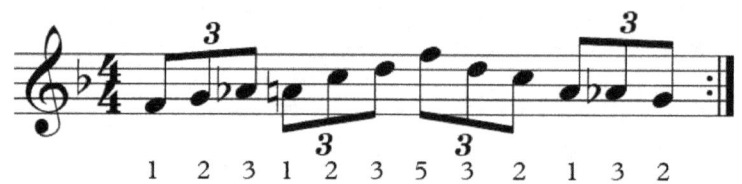

Major blues scale – two octave

F minor blues scale - six notes

Scale degree → 1   ♭3   4   ♭5   5   ♭7
                    (11th) (#11)

Minor blues scale – one octave

Minor blues scale – two octave

alternate descending fingering

ACCOMPANIMENT CHORDS FOR THE KEY OF F

1/7 chord shells

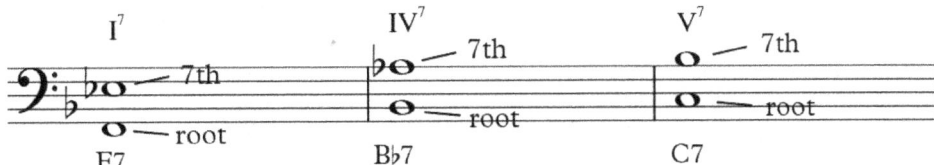

Guide tones

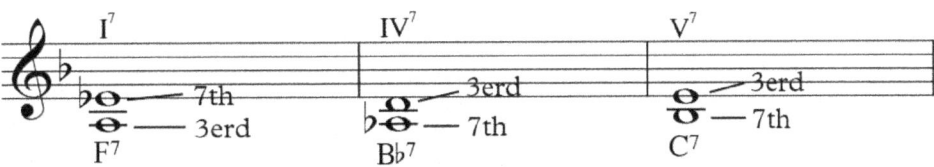

Inverted guide tones

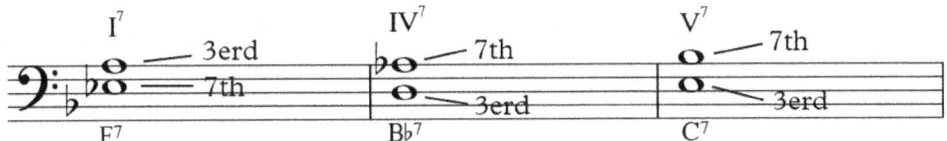

Rootless comping chord sequence A

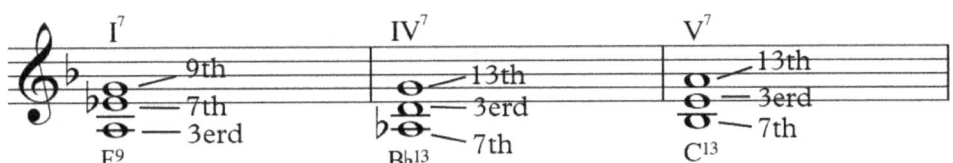

Rootless comping chord sequence B

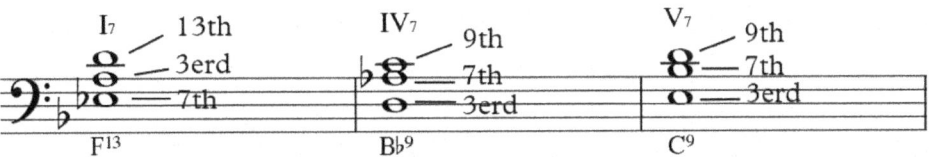

WARM-UP SCALES FOR THE KEY OF B♭

As previously mentioned, practice the right hand scale by itself at the tempo suggested (no left hand to start with). Once you feel comfortable with the scale try adding in the left hand shell chords –

♩ = 75-85

Major blues scale

Minor blues scale

Tune 49 (in B♭)

Track 95

See the following page for the analysis of this tune –

Tune 49 analysis

This tune switches back and forth between the major and minor blues scale several times and uses several added tones. In measure nine the scale changes to the F major blues scale (the root of the V^7 chord) for one measure. The ♭7 in that measure is the ♭7 of the F major blues scale.

Exceptions to not playing the avoid note over the IV^7 chord: notice that the 3^{erd} (D) is being utilized over the IV^7 chord in measures five and six (denoted as a diamond note head). As you know, that usually doesn't work to well. However, if played quickly (in this case as an eight note) you can sometimes get away with it. Here it is being used as a chromatic passing tone between the 11th and the ♭3.

I also want to mention that the right hand can be lowered an octave at measure eleven if you prefer –

Track 96

Tune 50 (in B♭)

There is a total of six added tones in this tune as indicated by the arrows. The tones added are the ♭6, natural 7, and ♭7. Go ahead and pencil in the tone names next to the arrows. The major blues scale is used for the entire tune. No extra analysis sheet is necessary –

BLUES SCALES IN B♭

♩ = 75-85

B♭ major blues scale - six notes

Scale degree → 1 2 ♭3 3 5 6

Major blues scale – one octave

Two fingering options

Major blues scale – two octave

B♭ minor blues scale - six notes

Scale degree → 1 ♭3 4 ♭5 5 ♭7
                      (11th) (#11)

Minor blues scale – one octave

Minor blues scale – two octave

Two fingering options

ACCOMPANIMENT CHORDS FOR THE KEY OF B♭

1/7 chord shells

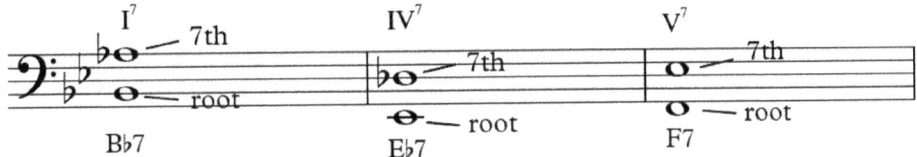

Guide tones

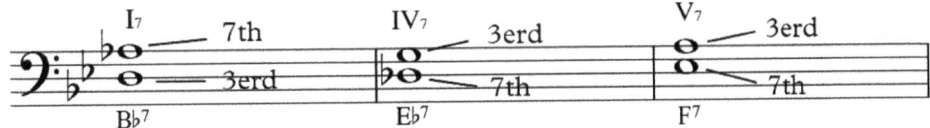

Inverted guide tones

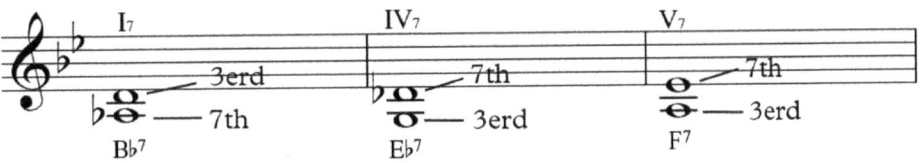

Rootless comping chord sequence A

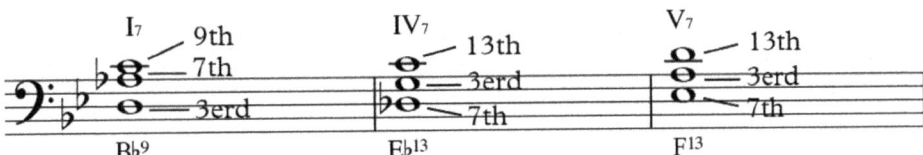

Rootless comping chord sequence B

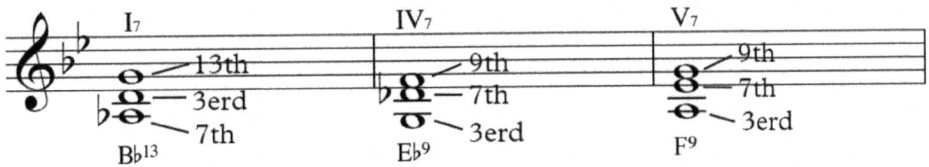

WARM-UP SCALES FOR THE KEY OF G

♩ = 75-85

Major blues scale

Minor blues scale

Tune 51 (in G)

Track 97

This tune uses the minor blues scale through-out with an added third. No extra analysis sheet is necessary –

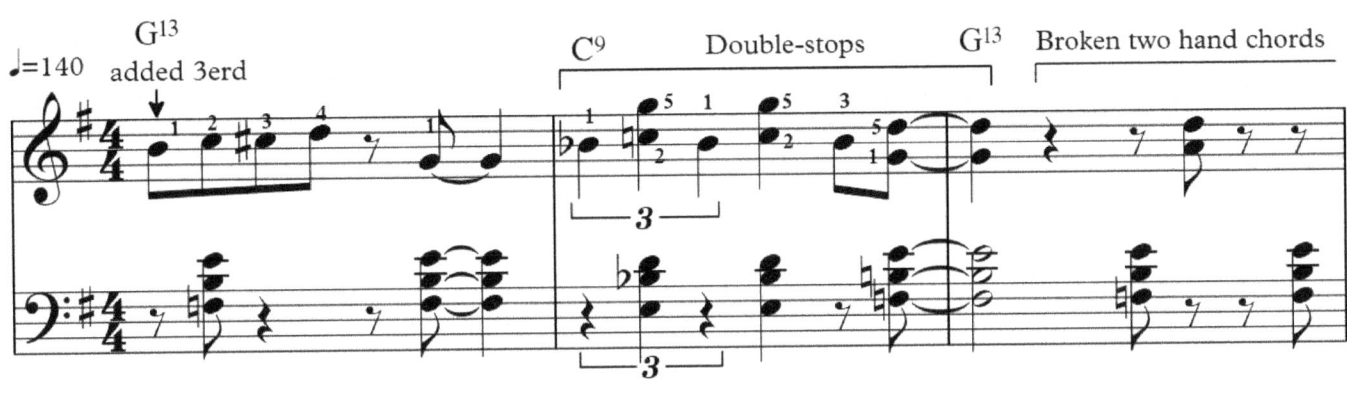

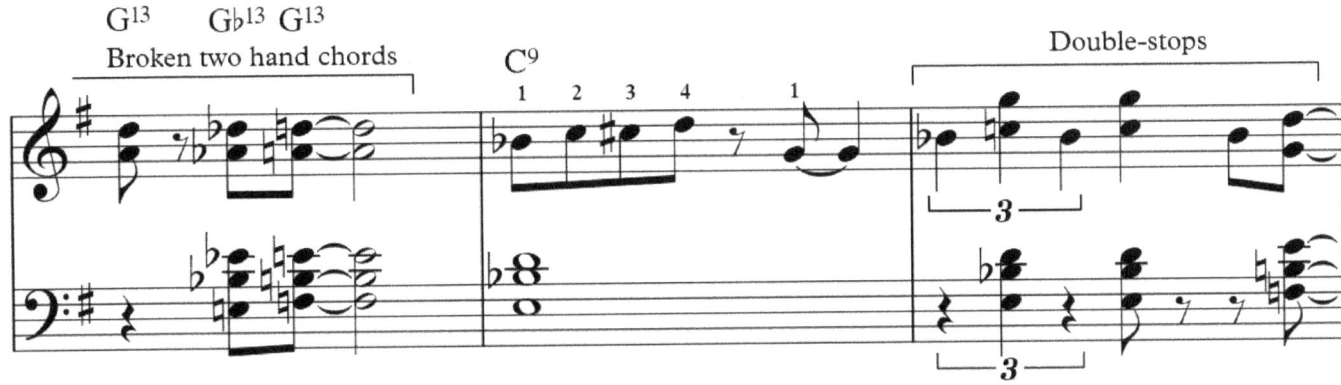

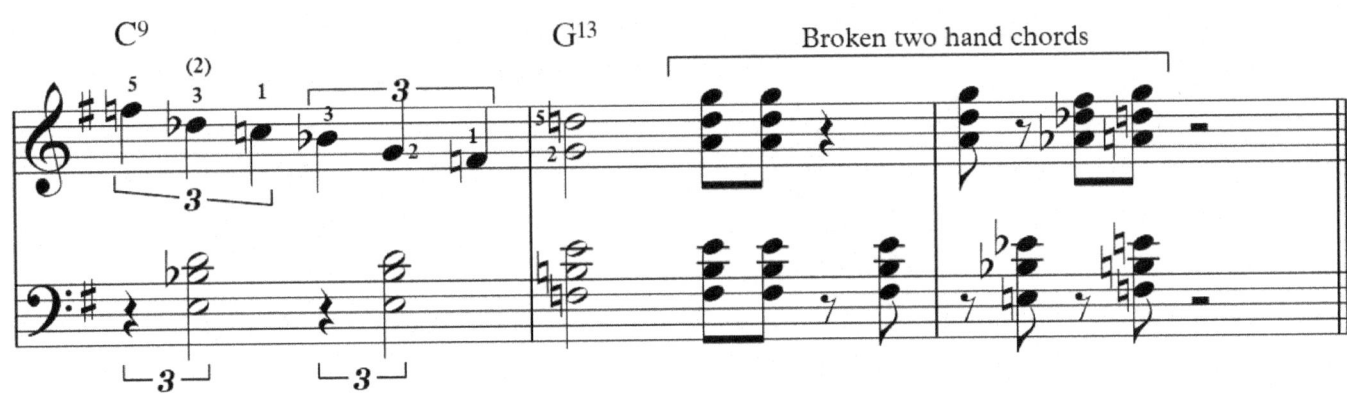

Tune 52 (in G)

Track 98

See the following page for the analysis of this tune –

Tune 52 analysis

This tune uses the minor blues scale thru-out with several added tones as indicated by the diamond shaped note heads –

BLUES SCALES IN G

♩ = 75-85

G major blues scale - six notes

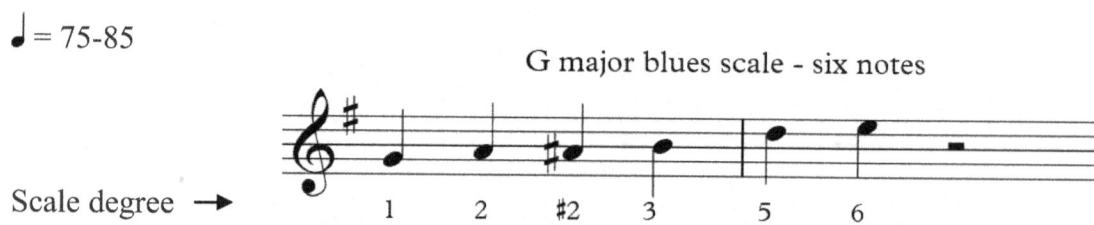

Scale degree → 1 2 #2(♭3) 3 5 6

Major blues scale – one octave

1 2 3 1 2 3 5 3 2 1 3 2

Major blues scale – two octave

1 2 3 1 2 3 1 2 3 1 2 3   5 3 2 1 3 2 1 3 2 1 3 2

G minor blues scale - six notes

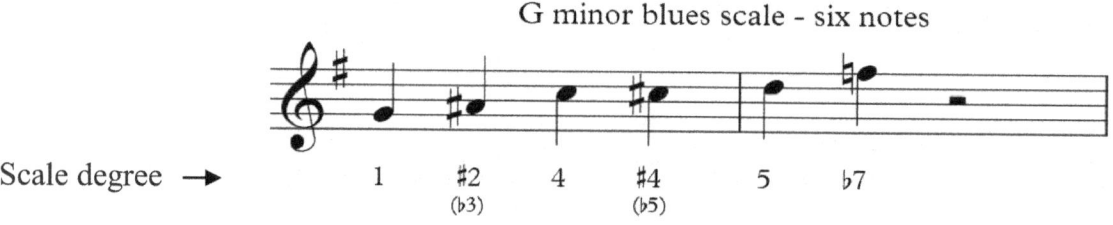

Scale degree → 1 #2(♭3) 4 #4(♭5) 5 ♭7

Minor blues scale – one octave

1 2 3 4 1 2 3 2 1 4 3 2

Minor blues scale – two octave

1 2 3 4 1 2 1 2 3 4 1 2   3 2 1 4 3 2 1 2 1 4 3 2

ACCOMPANIMENT CHORDS FOR THE KEY OF G

1/7 chord shells

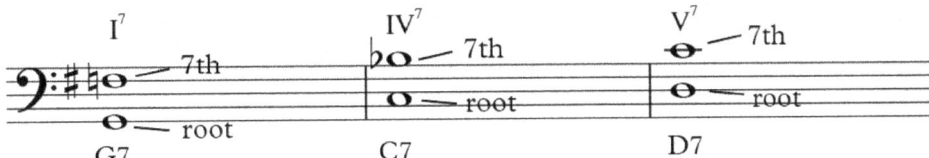

Guide tones

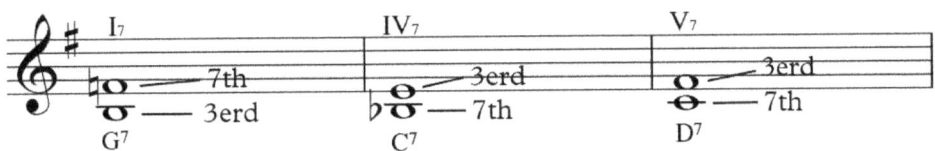

Inverted guide tones

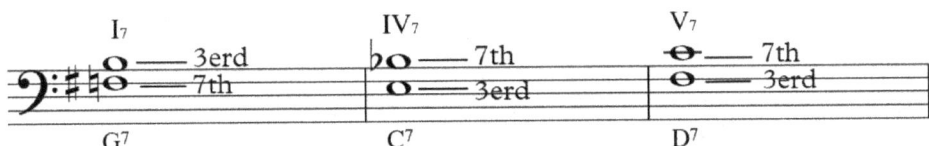

Rootless comping chord sequence A

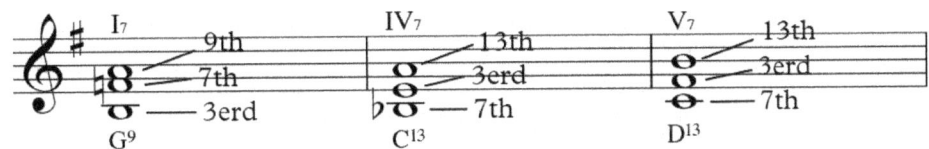

Rootless comping chord sequence B

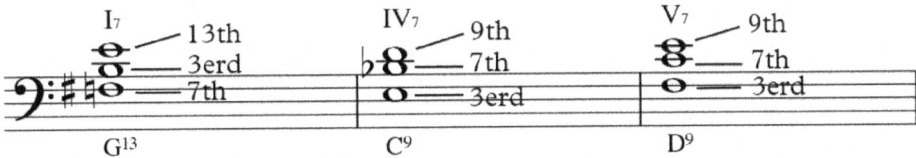

APPENDIX

Twelve bar composition template – top line for rhythmic pattern

Single bar rhythms for riff creation

Track 99 To create two bar riffs - combine two single bar rhythms

A little about me

My younger years
When I was about 12 years old and playing trumpet in the 6th grade my mother caught me writing one hundred times - I will not use my desk as a drum. This, at the request of my 6th grade teacher. Shortly after, I found myself taking private drum lessons in Thiensville, Wisconsin. After several years of private lessons and studying jazz drums at the Wisconsin College Conservatory of Music for a year, reality hit me and I realized I was going to have to work for a living. <u>Imagine that</u>.

Bread, water, and shelter
Coming out of high school the only thing I really wanted to do was to continue to play drums. Either way, a choice had to be made. Do I choose music as a career or do I get more education and go another route? To make a long story short, I choose the later and as they say, the rest is history.

The working years
Born in Milwaukee Wisconsin, I graduated from Milwaukee Area Technical College in 1980 with an AA degree in Electronic Communications and Broadcasting. After moving to Phoenix Arizona in 1981 I worked in the Microchip Industry for 4 years; Radio and telephone for 19 years; and 5 years in Air Quality; then retired in 2012. During these working years music took a back seat. From 1985 to 1992 I played percussion with the Scottsdale Symphony (a part time orchestra) and I would occasionally play drums for a jam session or gig. That was about the extent of my musical involvement.

The Piano
Even as a kid, I had always wanted to play the piano. In 1987, I rented one and began down the precarious path of learning how to play it. My method of learning was to go through various method books, DVD's, and internet videos that would show you how to play blues, rock, and other music styles. I did not use a teacher. It's not that I didn't improve by doing some of these things but my <u>progress was excruciatingly slow</u>. After fifteen years, I had improved only a little. A different approach was needed. That different approach came in 2005 when I began using an on-line teacher. This opened up a whole new world of idea's. Idea's such as as learning different ways to accompany with the left hand; learning how to play rootless chords; how to improvise; understanding song form and what tensions are, to name a few. And then – learn how to stitch all these idea's together in your own unique way that is your own personal style. This is a very different approach than simply improving your ability to read music. My reading has always been horrible and still is.

If you don't already have an on-line teacher (or live teacher) and are in a place you can do so I encourage you to try one. There are good ones out there. And then stick with it for a while. If you stay consistent and practice, you will improve faster over time.

To receive the audio tracks to this book or if you have any questions contact me at spiegeldan76@gmail.com.